FIRE IN TH

Poems 1955–1992

ERIC RATCLIFFE

♠

University of Salzburg

By the same author:

POETRY

The Visitation (Stockwell, 1952)
Little Pagan (The Poet, 1955)
The Ragnarök Rocket Bomb (Guild Press, 1957)
Transitions (Linden Press, 1957)
The Chronicle Of The Green Man (Ore, 1960, 1977)
Mist On My Eyes (Guild Press, 1961)
Leo Poems (Ore, 1972)
Warrior Of The Icenian Queen (Ore, 1973)
Commius (Quarto Press, 1976)
A Sun-Red Mantle (Mitre Press, 1976)
Nightguard Of The Quaternary (Outposts, 1979)
Ballet Class (Ore, 1986) (light verse)
Leo Mysticus (Astrapost, 1989)
The Infidelium (Astrapost, 1989) (light verse)
The Runner Of The Seven Valleys (Astrapost,1990)
The Ballad Of Polly McPoo (Astrapost, 1991) (light verse)
The Experiment ::
    Kingdoms (Astrapost, 1991); Hill 60 (Astrapost, 1991); Scientary
    (Astrapost, 1991); Ghosts Of The Quaternary (Astrapost,1992);
    Components Of The Nation (Astrapost, 1992); Ark (Diamond
    Press, 1992); Advent (Green Lantern Press, 1992).
The Man In Green Combs (Astrapost, 1993) (light verse)

BIOGRAPHY

Sheila Ann Ratcliffe 1949–1983 (With Vanessa Kembery: Ore, 1984)
The French King: Commius And The Legend Of Lear (Astrapost, 1990)
The Golden Heart Man (Astrapost, 1993)
William Ernest Henley (1849–1903): An Introduction (Astrapost, 1993)
The Caxton Of Her Age: The Career And Family Background Of Emily
Faithfull (1835–95) (Images, 1993)

HISTORY

The Great Arthurian Timeslip (Ore, 1978)
Winstanley's Walton, 1649. Events In The Civil War At Walton—on—Thames (scheduled 1994)
Megs, Roaring Or Otherwise, And Other Roarings (scheduled 1994)

ESSAY

Gleanings For A Daughter Of Aeolus: Essays And Poetry For Alcyone (Author, 1968)

PROJECTS FOUNDED:

Founder—editor: . *Ore* (1954, lapsed several years, recommenced 1967); *Ore Review Supplement* (1969, now incorp. in *Ore*); *Expression* (1962, as work of Whitton Poetry Group), title passed to New Richmond Poetry Group in 1964, ed. by Brian Louis Pearce 1965, 1968 ed. by Robert Druce and then by Leslie Surridge as *Expression One*, by 1970 had reached 22 issues; *The Druid* (1965, two issues only); *Six Hills*, newsletter and journal of Stevenage Poetry Group.

Poetry groups founded: Teddington Poetry Group, later as Whitton Poetry Group — a nucleus of The New Richmond Poetry Group founded by Brian Louis Pearce; Barnet Poetry Group, Stevenage Poetry Group.

FIRE IN THE BUSH   :::   ACKNOWLEDGMENTS

Some poems first appeared in the following publications:

Acumen, Artisan, Avalon Anthology (U.S.A), *Botteghe Oscure* (Italy), *Candelabrum, Chapman, Core, Corpus Journal, The Druid, East & West* (India), *Envoi, Epos* (U.S.A.), *Expression, Expression One, The Fiddlehead* (Canada), *Flame, Friday Market, Grub Street, Lynx* (U.S.A.), *Man!, Manifold, Moonstone, New Chapter, Orbis, Ore, Outposts, Poetry and Audience,* P.E.N. New Poems 1960, *The Poet, The Poet's Voice, Prospice, Quicksilver* (U.S.A.), *The Stylus* (U.S.A.), Whitton Poetry Group Collection, *Wisconsin Poetry Magazine* (U.S.A.), *Zebra.*

First published in 1993 by *Salzburg University* in its series:

SALZBURG STUDIES IN ENGLISH LITERATURE
POETIC DRAMA & POETIC THEORY

Editor: James Hogg

109

FIRE IN THE BUSH
Poems 1955-1992

by

ERIC RATCLIFFE
 barM

Institut für Anglistik und Amerikanistik
Universität Salzburg
A-5020 Salzburg
Austria

Academic advisers: Holger Klein, Leo Truchlar, Franz Zaic

Assistant to the editor: Sabine Foisner

FIRE IN THE BUSH: Poems 1955–1992

Copyright © 1993 by Eric Ratcliffe

ISBN 3-7052-0926-4

First published in 1993 by Salzburg University

Distributed in the United Kingdom by Images (Booksellers and Distributors) Ltd., 19 High Street, Upton upon Severn, Worcestershire WR8 0HJ

Distributed in the USA and Canada by Edwin Mellen Press, 240 Portage Road, Lewiston, N.Y. 14092 USA

"The whole Creation of fire, water, earth and air, and all the varieties of bodies made up thereof, is the clothing of God: so that all things, that is a substantial being, looked upon in the lump,   is the fulness of him that fills all with himself; he is in all things and by him all things consist . . . And of all those bodies that are called creatures or the clothing of God, mankind is the chief."

(*FIRE IN THE BUSH: The spirit burning, not consuming, but purging mankind*)

GERRARD WINSTANLEY, 1650

CONTENTS

The Maiden Of The Moon's Boat
Three For Vengeance
A Lady Kneeling For Holy Communion
Slave Girl
Lines For Any Dead Poet
The Golden Tempest
Elegy for My Uncle Buried At Girton
The Northland Men
The Unnecessary Silence
The Passing Of The Tribe

Leo Poems (1972) (p.67)

Parallel Travellers
The Photograph
On Words
On Air
On Light
Nurse, Teddington Hospital
Flower–Girl, Isleworth Hospital
Woman In The Train
Sestina For A Friend
Elaine
Thea
Jean
The Observer In The Train
Ashram
Prayer
Herb And Hooligan
Antelope Girl

Warrior Of The Icenian Queen (1973) (p.87)

Commius (1976) (p.101)

FOREWORD

I have never met Eric Ratcliffe, but I have been aware of his creative drive for forty years. In a necessarily brief review of his first published booklet (not included in this collection) I implied that his poetic technique seemed not yet adequate to convey the depth of his speculative lyricism. He must have forgiven this verdict, for only a year or so later I accepted his poem 'The Green Man' for publication in No.12 of *The Poet.* In the mid-fifties we contributed poems to many of the same magazines, both in Britain and America. Of those early poems I would pick out two which I believe are relatively timeless. I still marvel at 'Death Was No Empty Hat' for its originality and bravura. Now, several years later I would cite 'Nurse, Teddington Hospital' as best encapsulating all the positive force of Eric's spirit in a poem of triumphant affirmation that would not be out of place in a 1994 anthology.

He knew what he was capable of accomplishing, whether editors or reviewers recognised it or not, but little magazine editors were reluctant to devote space to poems occupying more than one page. In a 1955 note to me which has survived many purges of accumulated letters, he confided: "I would still like to write a long poem, but need sustained inspiration and no interruptions for such." How he managed to cope with the Porlock factor I would not know, but there is no doubting the sustained inspiration which drew so tenaciously on his passion for the culture suppressed by our Roman invaders. 1973 brought publication of *Warrior of the Icenian Queen. Commius* followed some three years later. Since then his narrative skill has gradually gained in assurance, leading inevitably to the planning of his most substantial achievement, *The Experiment*, first released in pamphlet instalments, and now collected together here for the first time. There ought to be a typographical equivalent of a fanfare!

I salute this major gathering, while happily noting that it is not by way of being a complete 'Collected Poems'. The Green Man has more up his laden sleeves.

Bill Turner

AUTHOR'S NOTE

In my experience as a small magazine editor, many poets encounter all shades of opinions of their work, as seen by the remarks of various persons quoted on pp.177-8. It might be right to search the minds of the least enthusiastic, in order to grasp a useful nettle. This is a more than perilous time to reveal poetry of mythical worlds, ancient history, legend and after-life belief to a majority of pragmatists and realists among readers and critics. However, on an opposite stage, much of the hard, brash, poetic fodder, in bookshops and known by performance work, denies aspects of human dignity and romantic idealism. It fails to satisfy those searching within a growing area of new faith in more spiritual matters. I am sure that a number of such people feel cheated when the market or bush telegraph does not allow their more discerning appetites to find enough work of poets of their persuasion. When they do, they must be delighted.

Without annotation, my more esoteric phraseology may only be clear to the converted. For instance, in *Components of the Nation.* Here in Section I the horse doubles for the human soul progressing on that useful glyph, the Tree of Life and "ultimate stardust" is the Kether state; the "divide" the horse jumps is the Abyss between the three supernal sephiroth and the other seven, six of which represent the astral, and the seventh our physical cosmos. The "coloured tossing" of the mane which whitens is equivalent to progress by losing wasteful emotional attributes. But quite a lot of my work is not so difficult to follow.

I am grateful to the publishers for supporting this first full-length collection; to Bill Turner, whom I lately discovered was still on this plane after publishing a very early collection for me in 1955, for a Foreword at short notice; and, as always, to Brian Louis Pearce through the years, who wrote a 28pp.'Appreciation' (*The Art of Eric Ratcliffe*) nearly twenty-five years ago, extracts from which are in Appendix A, for reader interest. Perhaps what matters most, though, is that some lines may give pleasure to those who discover them for the first time.

E.R.

LITTLE PAGAN

THE WHITE RIVER

In his dream he was again a shaking boy,
a sail blown on luminous waters,
a winking wraith following a white river
unwinding to an open jetty,
finding a vessel like a green thief

lying curiously in the shallows,
and a pale girl kneeling beside,
a playmate from the avenue of flowers
calling quietly along the white river
his forgotten name.

There was venom in the woman of wood
rising grey-handed from wind wilderness,
claiming his life and his small voice;
but the girl held out a prism of glass,
and in it he left two silver stars,

brothers to his twin young eyes,
while she flung roses rich as blood
into the ferry tide, to float with him
in the white river
for ever.

CYCLIC ADAM

In the land of fish and heron
and white candle maidens,
a dancing queen of five wings
collecting sea coral
in a wind of no purpose,
jumping by a lighthouse
discovered the Last Man
flat on his antique belly,
grotesque with wonder,
peering a stunted face
into rocking weeds
for gods and rare lights.

Afterwards from a tree
she noted his small teeth,
watching him stretching for nuts,
naked as a puma.

Hearing a temple bell,
she vanished in green dust,
breaking holy ampules
as a protection,
incase there were also serpents.

THE GREEN MAN

In the essence between dragnet day;
in the peace between dwale and poplar;
in the twig and near holy things;
by Earth's deep sluices; in enormity
by giant carving mandibles;
designing not hollow lust in the tropics,
night bells or juices of heaven,
but sweeping music travelling the winter
to a new cradle lapped in crocus;
knowing careful harlequin loins
stealing through blind, iron kingdoms,
and the regulated playfeet of topical ghosts
merrymaking in silver wilderness

- seeing in the shape of the fire downwards
a dead moth army, brother to brother,
yellow wings turning in corridor winds,
thinking arms bent like corn,
as the quail cries to the mirror water
and a throat splinters at time's end

- watching the boy with cherry-tree hands
set his sun-red mantle at summer
and hold to the lip of light his daughter,
a ghost star from a crystal girl,
a lover who climbed the western skylanes
homing a candle from her heart
at white harvest time

.... the Green Man.

His flagon eyes are ringed with hawthorn,
dew on glass spinning wheels
and guitars lost under the snowline:
boy and girl, armies and ghosts
who moved as threads through his blue mountains,
winged heathers and scattered waters,
now rest with the oracle of the rose,
asleep in his laden sleeves.

THE THROW

Barefoot on granite wait I,
who threw a silver javelin
into the shimmering land of whispers
and watched the wraiths divide
as though a chime had ended Hallowe'en.

Somewhere beyond the dawn a mermaid died;
the sea sent her comb to me,
with a wisp of her poor green hair
and a sigh for the savage who speared for fish
where white immortals moved.

NUCLEAR HERITAGE

High wings over the fox ferns
from meres of the morning star
in a singing brown man's dawn,
gods of six golden suns
quest the giant fish-catcher
by charcoal cross and thorn.

The pitted longfolded bones
torn from the last black pony,
dear follower of his destiny,
crumble on rainwashed stones
with pinions of steel angels
and iron of dead history.

Citadel and cold willow,
shuddered from blackened hills,
are dust to the sad seabirds:
the drawn hand on the longbow,
the full arm of the thatcher,
are twisted by dying herds.

There will be no more magic
by boar's head and yellow fire,
by hunting net and cauldron:
painful his round, wide eyes
under his mother's star;
shining, his spider children.

THE DREAMING TOWNSWOMAN

Young and pale her dreaming face,
seeing through her sleeping hands
a fine running singing man,
firm legs over the southlands,
the thirst of sun in his cobalt eyes,
sowing god seeds of silver
to reap moons of desires;
a singing man and his white mare,
free hooves timing a wild love tune,
great mane studded with firestones,
hurricane tail beating gaily:

a singing man and his white mare
and herself swung to the saddle
over the great mare's quarters:
he bringing her through the greenwood
to the hut by the leaning pine,
awake in his wide brown arms
– a wondering flaxen pagan wife
rich with the good sunlight....

Seeing the pavement sunlight
as a morning passenger,
she removed black April gloves,
glancing sideways at a police horse
and was concerned why it disturbed her.

DEATH WAS NO EMPTY HAT

Death was no empty hat, but a swung trapeze
    swept through a hall of song.
Hung on a silver wire, the winging bar
    leaped in a singing breeze.
Riding with woe, the sweet violins of home
    grieved in the high wall-lilac,
and the cadences of a shadowless piper called
    piteously from old pavements.

I heard, with the sighs of centuries, pagan notes
    whispering in the cupola,
and saw, in the flare of thunderhooks, scarecrow skies
    with wondering savage moons,
and a horn with flag ribbons blown by a coloured bird
    flying before my eyes.

THE RAGNARÖK ROCKET BOMB

THE RAGNARÖK ROCKET BOMB

The flat river-gods of Severn
have lost their whitewater silver
as holy by the wide sun-greenhouse,
the plants, his dear cherry guard,
the hunter has lifted a last arm
to his glorious festival birds:
flesh, steel, burials of history
are mixed with snake-green arrows
shot lightly from broken castles
by laughing, bright-bearded men.
It has broken the bones of buried playmates,
the flower girls of hard brown Britons
who marched with Arthur through cold meadows
with their border lanterns flaming,
the sweet, shy, sea-faced girls
who watched the thighs of the horsed warriors
roving with their high red swords.
It has broken the old breasts of boulders
where once in swift Welsh summers
the eye-gifts of the black jack-idol
bound to the grey rock gabbro
returned the sword thoughts of ancestors
who danced to the blood on his knees by lord moon,
who danced moongay with white nostrils,
who bellowed and looped between the ring-stones,
feeling their long sky fingers
beyond the arms of hot man-fires
riding to the unalterable god-eye
 socketed in black crystal;
who lay weeping beneath the wild berries,
left to the brook and the sleeping beaver
and the tall foreign church on the hill
as their wise grandfather's shadows
were walking the slopes of lost mountains
and the slender phantoms of Avalon

.guided the sick, golden Guinevere
down the sides of the great tor.
It has crushed the stone anchors of dead men
rolling in deep water-quarries,
and spilled from a sea-winking cradle
like a common tumbling sandboy,
the bones of a northland man-child,
a drowned prince of the blue swan-roads.
It has killed the rolling hound-bells
which have died crying Werberga's name,
screaming as they were pressed apart,
long clappers tipped like tongues
lolling in mouths of great iron dolls.

But I saw, dipping and designing
over blue shell and penny coral,
the light of a god walking the boundaries,
china-faced and luminous-handed,
searching for white spirits receding
from the craft of empy windmills,
stealing through spoiled, tumbled reeds,
fearing the whipping cat-blackness.
Because they had been held staring
with the fascination of being pulled
lewdly from some black swingabout
of a stag-beetle hanging lightly
in the embroideries of dark towers,
and had watched the fall-out dust
weeping slightly through these wind jesters,
they had left their bodies quite slowly.....
Yet something had been disturbing;
even from twenty-four hour bedrooms
the geometry of night-walks was distinct
and the three-dimensional pilots
walking the white clock hands
usually offered Freudian surprises.....

I, who had watched from slanting darkness
the naked minds in the dark, wounded furlongs,
queens bleeding in bitter hornwinds,
and the mile eyes of antique furies
gloating over the hemispheres of cerebral man,
waited for a god-breath from Snowdon,
for the jaunty legs of the men of Galway;
waited by brown terror hair
torn from a crag-born ice-woman
for cool winds over the failing birches,
the holy rock springs and the even seas;
waited, robin-eyed, for the short honey-insect
wending the clear long valleys;
waited for the scaring tiger-skirls of Man
looping the grey heathen skies –
when I saw from the fire-rim of broken marl
in the half-risen death of the amber summer,
six golden puppies twisted in their red blood
and a three-legged terrier taking a snarl
at the black legs of the whole world;
then I waited no more for Man.

Baby he was, who sipped the springing water,
the good drinker at the crystal fountain;
child he was, with the holy flesh
fed from the gazing stars above him;
boy he was, brother to the moon and lilies
and the great orange heart of the free summer:
he has dropped his iron cup,
touched the cambric at the end of time,
and floated with the scent of idols
far into the electric horizon,
the twisted vapour of a god's tear
which fell, and found no roots to cherish.

TRANSITIONS

SELECTIONS

THE SUICIDES

Shining in the good queen summer,
no mirror by the green wall ivy
would frame the shape of her tenderness;
into my hand she crept four fingers;
her name was written on the river
and this was her last act of worshipping.

Quiet as toys left alone in the darkness,
put down by the hands of great children
who chattered in cities beyond the waters,
with one phial for the three of us
we waited until the stars were faultless
and there was no wind on the cradle.

For a time we suspended our night forms,
seeing our heads like savage pottery
and the forking vine-green syrup
travelling on the rare surfaces;
then we rose in a kissing pattern,
a hollow hyacinth of three wraiths.

You will not hear from us golden songs
as we pass over still red rocks
when your pale daughters are sleeping;
we are the ghosts which bear no lanterns,
which are part of the wandering clouds
streaming between river and heaven.

LISTENING BOY

I was a giant who plied the free, bold hills,
with the heel of a hickory tree and a toy of iron,
and strode five leagues in boots of elephant hide,
when Jill was alive, and I her listening boy.

I was the fairy light of Will O'The Fen,
a hero of Troy, a lad with a magic kite;
I was the hen which sat on an eggshell world,
when Jill was alive, and I her listening boy.

I was the man who grieved to watch his friend
yielding her temple warmth to the mask of evening,
when she died, as the sun fades on a barley field,
with no word for her listening boy.

CENTURY HOUSE

The five-age walls feel the wind from blue waters
overhung in the cool witch-chimney,
and the ghost heart of a summer-wife, waking,
has recalled the sleepy fables
told all to the sun and her cradled daughters,
and how there was gold on the breast of a swanbird
when she sang to the river children.

She remembers the Easter firefly kisses
dancing from his dear lips,
and the two of them in the early shadows,
waiting bold as Welsh fairies
for moonlight over the dark home hills.
She has replaced the growing thorns
with roses of yesterday;
white as the leading phantom petals
she smiles through palace years,
and the wind from blue waters steals
to the thrush for her homely garden voice
– to the sundial for her tears.

OLD FRAGRANCE

Halting and walking in strange dead seasons,
through the weak lights of ghost Octobers,
surrendered to the final lute,
they sing from melodies unborn:

they have chanted how they remembered
the first sleeping diamonds of dew
on the white flowers left weeping
by the wall, in the graveyard dawn;

they have forgotten that instant without breath
in the green, midnight glory of cool ferns
– that moment in the lonely bedroom
when a whole heart sighed through curled fingers
and passed between two winds in the corn.

THE CHRONICLE OF THE GREEN MAN

On the cover of the 1960 printing are three candles, each one at a lower level, symbolic of the journey of Man into the unknown future, into the unknown depths, by the light of sense knowledge, or that which underlies the conscious activities of the brain. The poem is exceedingly concentrated in its imagery, highly geared metaphorically and symbolically, and probably needs a full key to its understanding. In the 1977 printing, the cover artwork was changed to include an illustration of the foliate head of the Green Man in the cloisters of Norwich cathedral.

E.R.

The Voices

MARY

JOHN

THE GREEN MAN

THE SPIRIT OF LIFE

THE SPIRIT OF THE FIELDS

THE SPIRIT OF THE TRIBE

THE SPIRIT OF PAST LOVE

THE CHRONICLE OF THE GREEN MAN
A Poem for Seven Voices

Theme: The sequence is best interpreted as a joint dream of two lovers, Mary and John, commencing and finishing in present-time – from the "hands of sunset" in their "mating south" to the awakening under Venus as the morning star. Though their Earth-bodies remain in the setting of their sleep in woodlands in summer, their dream bodies enter a new reality where the Green Man and the four Spirits tell them something of the panorama of life, love and death and tribal ritual before they awake with the lines starting "Under the silver light of Mary's morning star."

***

Mary
See the burning hands of sunset flare in our mating south:
the stars have eye-fever over the stark, whipped earth;
the grey north clouds turn through silver skies.

John
Be still, falcon heart.

Mary
In the whimpering light
where the lip of the drooping archway is the sky's love-line,
past the steel gantry, in the brain's brightness,
follow the stepping fox under saga moon;
share with his vixen the blood on the animals' footway,
leap generations to the younger Eocene,
read the leaves of the giant redwood,
see the animals rise in the moor's sunlight;
clasp the amulet, fear the tripping lake monkeys
and the light green birdweed of the live marshes:
follow the rocks to the stone woman.

John
To night, Mary,
your smile is mandarin.

Mary and John
We, who curved our veins to the blood's melody,
who lost the chatter of cities in the mind's mating,
have dreamhound power, and the mute thirst
of a black horse wheeling on thunderground
to plunge mounted down the hill's cape;
and the rider is ours, a mother-seeded ghost
night-born with the foxes from our twisted harlem bodies
as our scented mouths rhymed in the lonely lane,
our three-cornered hearts jerking like thinking boys.

John
The rider is ours,
tall, sky-human,
with a skin whip,
navigator eyes
blind with greater starlight.

Mary
Now, where the new wolds thin, our starchild is waiting,
as a weeping high violin sounds from an air-plateau,
and his twin young eyes are blind with the language of sea-
daughters.

Farewell to the fallen urchin rainbow
and the sounds in waterfront saloons;
to weed-footed men in cottage gardens
and the cold silt; to the walking sailors
and the songs of strangers by breaking seas;
to the lane's music and the morrow's day
threaded and thick with sunchildren;
to the rainboats on the common waters
and the pail's clatter by the animal farms
spread white on the green sliding lands.

John
Mary, flesh-sister,
raise sun-handed spears to the high rider.

Mary and John
From the honeycomb to the still lattice,
with bird-blood eyes looking outwards,
we are advancing from the live nest,
cortex-numb, locked, gibberhanded...

Mary
Like a hundred-head, in long swinging shadows,
we see eyes-between-trees
and torches, gaunt, red,
fanning bloodlight over old ridgeways.

John
Like a hundred-ear, jib-misted, listening,
we hear broken voices, coarse and murmuring,
and the black, tapping music of great fathers.

Mary and John
We hear dark lantern-shores issuing cold language
and the quick talking under trees of brown men,
whose fathers brough sandstealing boats from blue waters
and found the edge of a new wilderness...

The Green Man
Shivering and warm, like night-stallions,
they came to the brightness of hair-bright women:
whalebone strong in the shadow of ape-pillars,
stretched like filaments in the wind-white moon,
they made sons for the godfire dawn, and branwen daughters,
releasing eye whispers in the norm of night
from their lonely huts, to the trees of their fathers,
until by the blown air of the land's day,
in giant seas by green lamb-valleys,
opal as saints in the sandshore haze.
their beautiful bodies rose and turned,

bronwen-white, through the sighing waters,
as they breasted the waves to the breakfast-berry
with a wildflower from a Celt-faced hill.

Spirit of the Fields
Yet, not this only,
but ominous, white, silent singing
near hands born and risen for movement
in unsweet alchemy over the summer's late leaves;
and the universal teak trees stirring,
with the Great Hornbill to windward.

Spirit of Life
Then the long, low voices
in the Cave of Goats, molten and unresolved,
and the unborn foetus in the dark mother
waiting for that moment of the larch moaning
through the tired deadwind dawn,
and the red squirrel jumping the dewdrops.

Spirit of the Fields
And not this only,
but something heard by the white children,
bare as ivory under the roundhead sun:
something almost silent, something standing
watching the drum-sphere of Earth turning
and fernspike shadows creeping the screes.

Soirit of Life
Not like a greenchild
by doomlake, whistling in a poet's breeze,
watching the two white swans on the lake heart,
thinking of winter fountains, the rain of nightfall,
and long white horses passing under stars,
semaphoring the hung darkness.

Spirit of the Fields
Not like a heron-man

walking high in the thin, cooling wind;
not human, half-heard, unsmiling
and lever-legged below the arched thunder,
between the sea and the eastern rainbow,
fluid plains for her dominion.

Spirit of the Fields and Spirit of Life
She, white as limestone,
tipped like a truncheon from the Atlantic trench,
gazing to the memory of spires
early-headed in a welt of clouds
westward-born by a cycloid sun,
watching the trolling whale and the wide-footed trees.

The Green Man
The fairlight came with the animals:
from the lean bowhand to the low coast
the sky sang to the high hills of sunshafts on the lemon stones,
of a jackdaw on a golden scarp watching men palming raindrops,
of seabirds soaring the great cloud-corridors
over the labyrinth wombs of the pearled oysters;
of no dying under home stones for lone farming foxmen:
but of souls secure in nights of star-avenues.

Always the hands of gods have opened the stone recorders
and, for each cold heart, a swan in the western night
has flown between lanterns swinging in sorrow,
or has passed a black canoe on a weeping river.
So, dreaming, with green flying pennant,
the long shade rising one winter's year
from the heart-flesh coiled in the knight-grave,
saw hillside wreaths roofed where the bird-tones
leaped the brown towers and tall holy grass.
He remembered the bones of his five sun-oxen,
under alligator lands of the new men;
the animals which had carved their earthlines
after stumbling dust-hooved along drinking tracks
to the sparkling calf-milk of round, cool lakes,

with tiny stunned flames in their swinging copper heads,
like tight, savage suns from a brass noon sky;
hearing always the call of the squat, silken water
singing low like some sweet, rough mother...

Time once slowed to the gliding danefire
closing the misted worlds of gowned rivers
as he rowed by the secret songs of bowmen
to the glamour tide riding the low wick
by the long, open light of his own harbour:
home was the walking of two tall daughters,
the fine play with their toy rocking falcons,
and the eyes of goddesses on his clay walls
watching their faces turned to the white dogstar.
Now fire and frost were the same thing
to his Saxon wife, hard as a figurine.
who spilled into fog near the fairies of the hill
where Balder's mountain light sunned Yggdrasil;
where murmurs hollow as white moonbeams rose
through the corngrowers crying in the long death-night.

Spirit of Past Love
Where was this long-armed girl he fetched from the field,
who knelt for the priest with the silver boat-bowl,
with her blue singing-bird, and her great bride-crown
– this little maiden-bud, with the light tokens?

Spirit of the Fields
How did she wander with ghosts in the lifting wind,
when fire and frost were the same thing,
with her dayfire gone, and the wand of her white arm
a weak as a twig on a mountain-birch tree?

Spirit of Past Love
Now her small hands sleep by the young dog-rose
pressed in the cold thighs of giant's clay,
and the strings of travelling harps of iron strangers
will not strike for the bare, long, loving arms

of she who cradled music in the old day
and once filled the drinking horns of song-dancers.

Spirit of the Fields and Spirit of Past Love
O ring the Abyss, dark Sister of the Bells;
turn the hot stones by the legs of the fire-elves:
once she took his voice to the stars,
once he was with her on the Honey Island.

O ring the Abyss, dark Sister of the Bells;
lift her young crystal on four white ferns
to a far singing by island flowers
springing near eastern sun-fired barns.

O ring the Abyss from your silver arcades
with the songs of the holy birds of Rhiannon:
search for her face dropping low by the wolf-trees;
search for her face near the long fire movement.

Spirit of Life
In a high morning, on a high hill,
the knights will break their banners by the evergreen,
and the enigmatic blood of lost battles
will again be moist each side of the open road;
and those who were loved will be lost in the midnight earth;
those who were feared will walk by the fringing trees
In a high morning, on a high hill.

The Green Man
Night without song, hyaena night
and low skeinwind thrilling the green-printed ground:
night without song, with the father breezes
strung from the stars to the glinting moonberry:
night without song by the reptile shale,
by the blood, the apple, the windflung nectar;
by strike bats poised under curving moons.
Light without song, light by the great rock
where day was sweet on the sheltered side,

where life was good and the maple opened
and the foetus was saved from blindness.

Day without song, stag day, hound day
white with the sun of unborn Easters,
with weight-walking animals crossing the plains
– until, on the wide green monoland eye,
sunk in the soil by the green tree-forms,
primeval giants with splayed fingers
pushing the early stalks to the sky
saw the first haired woman watching the condors
who, raised in the wracked light from slow gibbon walk
and taken by bullmen looking for morning wells,
found their half-iron bodies sweet as Heracles.

Spirit of the Fields
Was this a hollow woman
brushed by the bees and the incense of flowers,
not with a high spring face and fragrance,
but hollow-mantled like a dry sun-stalk
with the full animal in her maze eyes?

Spirit of Life
Was this a stone woman
under the same stars as the thin fox,
not like a green-sexed willow girl
ripe with a smile and pan-lullaby
but colder than berries by the whiteheart tree?

Spirit of Past Love
Curve her proud back to the eastern sky
to be kissed by the cross-silk sun
like an Indian dreamer with lantern eyes
seeking a south-high flower wife.
For when her tiger nail is indrawn
and she follows her mate with a long, dark smile,
and the river has risen for the fires and the nightfishing,
the harp of man will come to her fingers...

And when she threads the fire-twisting night
to play to her brown children,
through the weeds of the magical river
sweeping the long blue waters
will gaze the beautiful totem face
of Ishtar, the maid of the moon.
As the song of her harp honours the sky,
singing red through the hard slave wind,
all will be beauty and the fields green
through the smoke of the burning of grass,
soft and wild the piping of girls...

Spirit of Life
Risen from the great slime nucleus,
cousin of water molluscs,
was she dark under May-moon skies
with a glistening lover near the rain-lanterns?
Twisting and creeping to slake her lips
parted like water emeralds,
was she sinuous by night-green trees,
flexing her smooth lake-limbs?

Spirit of Past Love
O my heart, there were flowers in the wildwoods,
winter-white her spirit and cool her brown hero;
bright was her moonwaist thrown on an oak branch,
light as a rainbow loved from the sky
as a leaf shivered once.

The Green Man
At moontime on the path of the sandbird
she weaned her china-human son
as green hands of sea-moss cradles
grew from the slow receding tide;
and greater than the branch-hopping birds'
were the cable arms of her motherhood,
loving where the hare turned to sleep,
firm when the spearheads with wings

were thrown by the cold starwaters.

Stretched on the folded ferns,
she bore her spring-handed daughter
like a gentle seed at sundown
when the voices of men in war-black ferries
were songs from the sons of thunder
and the high sea-beacons were savage.
Under the silver light of Mary's morning star
her four-winded dales were summernight cathedrals,
and all the mile orchards a lattice for gods' blue tears.
Her love was an insect caught in an amber island
where the notes of the sun-linnet knew no sorrow
and evening ravens in queen-eyed summers
watched the Saxon barley girls.

Spirit of the Tribe
Look back to the tears of Isis, Emmanuel,
to the years of the starnight floods;
look back through moth and the tomb
to cannon-blood and gold and bluecloth maids
and diadem berries lemon as queens.
In an old water-dream with the hands of the tribe,
look past your grey north tower in the chanting light:
through milk and the womb
dance, dance and twist by the high man-stone.

Black was your maiden;
as wide as a hand her golden hair-plates.
In the arm-curved light
her token was music from the coloured water globes.
Yours the white face in the kitten corn,
yours the legs of the long men of the hills
dancing to the piping in the thicket.
Timeless and rare,
yours the voice from the glass mountain.

42

The Green Man

By dragon's road and hollow,
climb the hill to your fern-headed master
- the root-footed, the cup-bearer, the refresher.
You two are one, your brow and your tongue
are the sky and the mountain river moving through holy shadow:
see, you grow as wide as two forests
- a scarf of trees around your body,
and all the animals are in your blood.
Take the axis of your heart, and by the hindlight
revolve thrice. You are the green universe and its owner,
you are its sons and daughters.
In the channel light, which is also green,
you are birth and death, Emmanuel.

The Spirit of the Tribe

Remember your lover-hands drifting through the night
and your torpid words to her
like small worlds on that evening sea
which lay around your melancholic boat:
lest you be afraid, she is not lost,
for many are the dreams from the night-handed watchers
who rise behind reflections in the wine,
who guide the sleepers from the unreal day
by hollow-sounding lyre, haunting eye,
and the long grieving voice
- whose flickering hands, whose evening gems
make delicate your sleep.

The Green Man

The skin beat, the hand upraised at the altar;
the drumbeat and the strong body movement;
warriors' twist and peasants' nod
- these are the essence of communication
as Man in the emerald of his static world
is urged by continental forces.
His brain sweeps behind cabin-eyes;
he watches the plum and the merryweather;

then, like some heavy.silver firefly, vanishes,
and is remembered as that flock-headed wanderer
once tented under the long smoke
by the long tomb and the waterway ferry.
But under the last sun, no merlin man will eye
the bent twig, the blue sky leaning;
or beneath an apple-tree a silver lady
spread like a white moth her lovely form:
under the last sun on the brigand-green waves
the helical cobra will writhe upon the waters
as the last man's face grows sinister
and his white lady's song, like a listless ship
is of love unknown, the pilot dead.

By flag, pennant, wide, hollow shells
and the working arms of grey machines,
the tribe's music stirs, gathers, points
to suns embedded in a lyric sky:
but at world's end time, by the broken juniper,
at the time of the spilled greenblood,
all will rise like Arthur with his new Mary faith,
shedding their brief blossoming bodies
by low rushes and Himalayan lichen;
and she with the shining eyes, at world's end time,
will put through that darkness, death, her silver hands,
as over the free mists his wise summer-form
leaves the dead legend wings of the ivy-bird
which once ringed the world from his hands' hollow
- leaves the green lily, the man-tree, the slow blood oxen,
until, slender-legged, they stand by a gold river,
with no folly in their arms.

***

John
Under the silver light of Mary's morning star,
we are the lovers with temple hands

holding the Everlasting Man.

Mary
Holding the Everlasting Man,
we stand with a smile, facing the seasons
– our backs to the April tree.

John
When we are old children
and youth rises from solitude
and the brother wind dies on our faces,
we will place the golden cradle
between the lavender and treasure-towers.

Mary
In evening-coloured union
as we walk like Palmer's people
through the straight and homely dusk,
the songs of the Great Mother
will call us to the sun:
the singing of the Queen of Heaven.

John
Be still, falcon heart.

MIST ON MY EYES

THE COMING OF THE TRIBE

Under star-clusters in the shell night
my gipsy god is riding in silver
over white auras of sleeping girls
and brown boys, charmed to awake
when the hawk-sun warms their eyes.
He will feel the soft coming of voices,
bell tones creeping by red shores,
the movements of tiny-handed rainbow men
toiling on their farms in the blue air.
He has known the amulets of kings,
the drifting cherry clouds of cool evenings
passing over pure milk rocks,
the worn trackways of old flintmen,
the quicksilver of death, the longbarrows
near great moons heavy as amber
– steady entombed wrists of marble
crossed in patience under revolving winds
– the lanterns of a thousand decades
like pinflames before the sun's corona.
From the heart of a cooling galaxy
he has built with hands of crystal
the twin white pillars of Man and Woman:
to their temples over the swan roads
he has given his blessing.

ROMAN SILCHESTER

The old carrier wind has passed the bushes,
iridescent, set rare as pagan brooches
firm in the dress of the blonde moonfield
glinting with night jewels like a crescent,
where shivered flintlight is starpointed.
Wrung from the flesh of the Atrebates
the round brown weaver trees have sprung
deep through the powdered Belgic frosts
to the magic loom of the Silchester night,
while Calleva covered the birds which sang.
And the birds which sang were like the lovers who loved
or the tall brown fruit girl of the Forum
who knelt to Heracles in pre-Wessex sun
and prayed for the strength of the new men-children
she would give to time and the flowers.

Here, where the gaunt tree-gnomons reach
we are not far in time from those old poets
who sang of the colour of beautiful women,
woven cherry-fire in their harvest faces,
blood-snow in their winter skin:
here I will tell my last love, with her grave supple body,
when snow is melting or in winter sunlight,
"They are not the winds on the rivers or ghosts in the skies;
they live in our lonely hearts and our twin-made eyes,
though Calleva has covered her children."

THE GRAIL

For water-roots and branches of sparlight
and birth on the slanting stairs of the sea
I lent birdwing eyes to the new night
to seek the wonders by a sacred tree.

From the luminous boughs, eerie with power,
like past faith walking an old swan-lane,
bright as an ice queen from her bower
Blanchefleur stole through a mist of rain.

Sleeved in silver and fountain-blue
her wand-white arms signed through the ether
and over her talisman-hand she flew
a veil as green as a holy river.

From the amoured ring of the roundflame dawn
the sword of the hawk-sun pierced the veil
and under her talisman-hand was born
a Child of Light from the ancient Grail.

I brought birdwing eyes from the old night
which had sought for wonders by a sacred tree,
like water-roots and branches of sparlight
- and birth on the slanting stairs of the sea.

MARY AND THE MILLWATER BELLS

Awake to the hour,
breathing to the window-moon saint, to the silence of outer
      phantoms,
my clean body hears the sly lean rain on the daffodil leaves:
if the millwater bells chimed now, God would walk to-night
- a cool, turning, white bird - and light running upwards from the
      dew-violets
would hang like a river of blossoms over ghosts by the cold trees
- waiting as oval-faced water waits for sun on its sleeping swans.

This was my body,
in dream maner discovering dimensionless reality, touching fairy-
      blood,
feeling sliding fintails of mermaids with wide Turkish kisses
or thieving wild wood in night-velvet from the June legs of tree-
      daughters
for a brown harp on its strong shoulders strung with green
      weeping vine:
sleep singing under sleep,fingering hurtling tunes in the she-light;
sleep measured by unseen stars, counted in golden calendars.

When I meet Mary,
my bones will be new in the clean-angle mornings of sauntering
      day-worlds;
these brown fingers could rock like dumb little men along the
      pavement,
writhing to cock wiry salutes to her white festival skin.
Under the bending smoke of fire, when you're an old god for a
      poet, Mary,
think of me who sighed verses for your ghost's garden,
who wove a curtain of gold for the last act told to the still bare
      blood.

Will you remember
your youth, Mary, when your high, mad hair shakes in the
    moonlight?
Will you remember, old one, that the skull is the prison and not
    the prisoner?
Too soon, then, you'll take my green arm, unfurled to the dawn,
for your dear hanging soul - a valley of stones for your poor
    pilgrim atoms
to be scattered by whirlwinds on warrior bones and the old sand-
    tigers:
too soon, those giant white clouds will take your wild eyes
    from me.

Do you remember
the day pining, with its hands folded, watched by the buttercups'
    Ganges eyes;
the night-lily, waiting for us to go, after nine hours in the furze,
and a great haze stealing from the west through the open vedantic
    evening
to our temple in the recircling breezes, sun-spire dominant?
Then, on the air-stirred earth, you were the movement of all
    beautiful women,
the maple-cheery girl - the traveller under the head-dress of the
    south wind.

Who taught me to dream?
It was my mother, watching the light pools in my small round
    eyes;
resting my young face between the stars and the slipper
    quartermoon;
singing of sun-fields, gemini creatures, and the voices of silver
    birds.
If I sleep now, perhaps her hand will haunt my hand's hollow,
    beating slow music,
and, under a scarlet tree with a fire-girl's skin, Mary will grow
    younger,
and I may hear a echo from those millwater bells.

FOREVER

Long, long ago, before the puffin swam,
neither sun nor sail bewildered those
who, simple in their sleep, walked to a day
of golden trees and apples in the air,
and quiet, tilted villages.
The men flailed and the women wove
and when the eyes of heaven closed
they rested by fin-fairy fires
and watched the smoke climb upright to the stars.....
Here the peace of an eternal autumn passed,
still leaves endured, and for the steeple doves
time kissed lightly undeneath the moon
as the stones of ancient masons sang
the pale language of the living dead;
the wall chants of the spirit of the race
who left his talismans at eventide
lonely in the grey home shade.
Here lay the axe, once sun-slanted and crossed
before ripe muscles on a summer morning,
and the old stones sing back two thousand years
to the skin-belted body turned in the sun
which twisted and struck, one lever of flesh
at the tree on the forest floor.
Only the blue flints know of the heavy dead
fibre-bare in the deep midnight earth,
under the dumb centuries of cloven hooves,
and of their souls' last kisses before they fled,
like shadows on the arms of some star-white god....

Forever beneath the high moon clouds
the red-haired cattle stray,
meeting and passing like porcelain
upon a waxen way.
Sires of their sires by hecatomb
had writhed beneath the sun

– some new man-woman would bleed
the calves of their calves by gun;
and one dozen paces from their skulls
would meet in temples on the shale
– with hassocks at their feet.

STOLEN PROPERTY

Pure and cold, superimposed upon the man, straining,
the legs of the sky came down upon the woman:
a white star entered: satisfaction was effortless;
delight like rice being poured in the hands.
So, seeded in shade, or the limelight of dawn,
the curved loins of the daughters of men
steal more than the sweat of passion, siftings of flesh,
but take to the womb harp-calls, summer lightning,
odours of trees in rain, some lonely star.

Opened and dark by the nettle roots are the sallow faces
and my dead shrunken mother in the earth's sluice;
the flower her haven, the delicate mould her shawl.
         She stole once....
the sight of may to quicken her spinal young god, stirring,
the look of leaves before the morning sun
to bring shadows and lights to him,
the mirror's glance at her womanhood to show him Columbine.

Gentle in my cells now, stealthy as the pale air,
I hold her green blaze in my son's head:
though moons move blind to my eyes across the boundary land
bearing my bitter daggers of blank bone,
I, under the night's fist, alone, far in earth's chemistry,
will have sold her sins - bright thefts guilty as love.
So here I leave the impulse of her images for you to steal,
perhaps to add to the delight of some white star;
you, an unknown sweetness of a foreign mind.

THE GENTLE RAIDER

The Viking crouched once:
he saw his rovers darting like death fairies
from the black oars of his long dragon-boat,
hiding hip-low in the dry beach cave;
he was the metal cage of the walking Northland
waiting where life was pure as an air-mirror,
where the English birds were breaking the eastern morning.
watching sun-trails with an iron stare,
looking for careless lovers on the lean south lands,
his face a flame, his mind a valley burning
as walking women under travelling skies
gathered green spices from the wide sea-tors,
laughing like villages of dreamy giant-eyed children.

The Viking crouched once,
a red wish in shadow as the clean light failed,
foot-fierce on the flank of a farm whelp, dying,
crying a faint crooked howl to Alfred's Hill;
and when the blue Saxon midnight met the sea,
under the high apples and the dancing stars
he crept like a doll of steel from a small owl tree
to where the fire of a field-bride opened its heart
and the stretching firs were a part of her brown flesh
branched bare in the hanging nightwind;
and he bound her sweet hand blossoms with goblin ivy,
took her summer gold, and his gay sword
held her scream quiet in her waking breath.

The Viking crouched once,
and lifted her down to the sad sea rocks.
To his grey fortress in the Northland dawn
he sailed the girl Saxon with her summer gold,
and her mystical cries fled like singing glass
on the Celtic waves, as his dragon-boat passed,
and her shining tears dropped on the hunter waters

as she bent an arm to summon a fighting man
and a cold monk's wind from the shores of Ethelburga.
At the end of the great swan road, in Saxon surrender
she sank to his deep chest like a white psalm,
where his river had three hands, and one was slender
as a blue palm closing on a swimming star.

THE MAIDEN OF THE MOON'S BOAT

Behind these yellow leaves I see the maiden of the moon's boat,
her smile straying, her light throat bent over the path of
  suffering.
Inside a convent of trees she rides, the Bride of my God,
floating a silver mile below her shining side,
as I, like these many branches, open my heart to her.

THREE FOR VENGEANCE

Slowly burning my altar candles
I had thought of his horned hands
and his hard round skull;
how, clasping her amulet in the night pit,
brown on flower bed under his rock form,
she had defied him.

Pointing my dreaming arm over an earth–tower
I saw a black star with the marks of numbers,
and his was Three:
the moon-goddess showed me three Chesil stones,
and, chanting my fury to the wine air,
I slung for his blood.

High, twisted high, I carried him,
the north wind in his wide face,
to the White River;
then under a sacred tree I laid my dead girl,
and out of ivory made an angel bird
to live with her softly.

But when the sky spirits flung light,
shouting across the waters her great name,
I saw its young wings rise to the sun,
quivering, as her hair turned gold,
to my lost voice.

A LADY KNEELING FOR HOLY COMMUNION

The red heathen faint beneath her skin, she kneels;
dark as a pagan arrow shaft the shade around:
nightbrush, God in a myrtle tree, the wine of wonder;
    all three my delicate lady.

The bird in her curved eye, grey and lively, rises
in troth to bread and the holy goblet:
beautiful peasant, moon-made and carnadine;
    both my delicate lady.

Hers the vision inward, substance of love luminous,
sun on western fields, the smile of Glastonbury,
bird-call, hill-shine, this maid of St. Bride for all,
    all my delicate lady.

SLAVE GIRL

A low arrow, I search the land
for her silver feet moving leaves
as she follows through spiced fields,
runs, or turns to a bird cry.
My father brings an iron whip
to make her lie with Usnach
who will clasp her roughly
in a dark night without singing.

When she feathers her dawn hair
by the eyes of glittering wells,
I will give her holy corn,
my mother's summer gold
and a five-pointed sea-spear
to help her defy them
who steal near young mountains
like shadows of evening panthers.

LINES FOR ANY DEAD POET

A giant in his tears, dumb to the ears of men,
he leaned, splay-fingered, in snowbird silence:
out of the swung mists and from his bedshadow
under his fatherland stars he asked the flowers
the secrets growing in their tilted eyes.
All his, once, the wind's rock, the tripod lock of roots,
the petal whimper, the starting sap and swept impulse,
the tiny triggered senses.

The black roof rains have smoothed his sculptured footprints,
but in his five dead hearts rest highland silver,
musk, moon and granite and a greencup flower;
for in his candlewhite heaven the clouds have kind faces
and each new voice a heart.

THE GOLDEN TEMPEST

The trembling fern-moth, settling wings on sandstone,
weaver of ghost tissue from each mountain wind,
has seen the eye of the ringed morning lizard,
and the carved kingpost, high in a sacred summer,
now lamenting to its grey bird, the perching falcon,
has flickered the tongues of dreams across a siren sea
to a land laden with breathing, to the living air
around black stallions and their golden warriors.

The scrolled shapes of the stone fathers of the land
front the tor, six faces blind as stars,
as in from the coastal mist, over the heathen marshes,
comes a chorus of sable fingers, glistening, turning,
rings rolling like golden eyes in a mantle of thunder.

O then sand singing quietly, humming from unhewn stone,
as if a woman standing by sunned magnolia trees
lightly strummed her zither to a wild holy world ....

O Bird God, in your onyx eye the firewind is growing
as you carry a yellow wand in claws of bronze:
far over old green anchors and deep sea moss
take a sevenfold crown to first man on his crag,
and across the wide silence a golden heart
to beat under leaves by time-counted skeletons.
When the albatross over his granite has wheeled no more
and the blood on his great stone axe under the moorland
has been forgotten, though men die sightless,
through faithful hearts they will see him again
clung to the scarp, with the wind in his ageless hair
and his high fires flaming to hunter moons.

ELEGY FOR MY UNCLE BURIED AT GIRTON

Old county sailor, has the sea-sun lost your brow;
free to be indecisive, strange in a land,
do country voices spice your thinking now?
What human star-eye from the past, what hand
of secret silver, what grandeur guides your prow?

Eyeless ranger in a fire-gaunt haven
or bitter harvester on formless earth,
are these holy things that you have chosen
or motor pulses of unsaintly birth
behind our twilight tapestries, Christ-woven?

After this midnight, may you recover the straw dawn
and your own tall pages in fay-edged history books,
and by the shelves, rayed in the lily-light cone,
find a companion like a legend looks,
telling of brides and hunters to be born.

When priors of space and time advance their crosses
to long white men who crystallise their flesh,
what hills, what singing earths collect the losses
of those who see their friends pass through the mesh
of green and silence underneath the mosses?

THE NORTHLAND MEN

Of the northland wind
I told my green daughter,
and of the red wine
that sometimes came down
from broken men:

To the northland sky
through a vertical sea
she rode six glass fish
and saw boats sinking
to my open caves,

– the northland men,
their melon-headed bodies
shrugged with water,
turning and chasing
on walls of waves;

but the northland night
was pale with stars
and golden faces
and the travelling hail
was sudden with light:

down the vertical sea
her green hands whispered
to the ocean floor
"Sea-god father
they are greater than we."

THE UNNECESSARY SILENCE

From embrittled pasturage, between the night lungs of their fires,
old monastery and daffodil, men build churches and their spires:
like slipper ferns which seek the sky, they fly these holy kites to
    God.

Their corn-legged daughters were not made to vagabond before the
    tomb,
whose solar substances inlaid the salt and moonwater of womb,
who show the fading lantern image of those once born to paint the
    sun.

Ceres brides to mandrake, acorn – the glowing oak for master,
confused by myth and statuary, by a flowing sense chimera,
they dance and twist in helices; in tango light they run.

who like temples from the depths of water-green were won,
misunderstanding, turn stone to iron, copy in glass the sky;
misunderstanding, mantle flesh and mechanise the lie.

who like artists from the flaxen land should rise to paint the sun,
misunderstanding, by coins and sudden numbers perpetuate a
    ritual;
misunderstanding, forsake for merchandise the symbol-lovely
    petal.

So who would say that it would be Unnecessary Silence,
if, misunderstanding, God should staple back their flesh to earth;
misunderstanding, fuse groin to groin in blinding thermal death.

THE PASSING OF THE TRIBE

Leaving my helmet on shale,
I will stretch my brown right hand,
taking a sword out of mist,
a cold limb from a hollow sea.
Though with my sword I would be one other
clashing through singing thunder,
ringing steel orchards,
simian I will come to a grave,
kneeling to a lament of spears,
remembering by green music
how children of my lemon land,
praying into the heart of night,
put out pinniform arms to the stars
and whispered of avenues of roses
– how sunlight failed the good pear tree
and country virgins knelt their eyes
from milk and corn to golden woodflame
– and the shy, lame man who smiled at me
from a circle of quiet fires.

LEO POEMS

SELECTIONS

PARALLEL TRAVELLERS

Like twin stars on the sky's base,
parallel travellers are to each objective;
the end of the journey is a meeting place
and the act of travelling is subjective.
So, whether from Wales or Iceland you write your letters,
the country is limbo but the paper sacred;
and substance is absent from our moving fetters
though the trackway terminus is consecrated.

As an open surface, dust-white in the moon,
your essence is the essence of silent space,
prepared for god-shadow or some early rune
to be scribed on a resting monolithic face.
But this of yours, like air under summer stars,
brood of colours born in a bowl of glass,
or smoke of wizards curling from magic jars,
– defines no regions to enter or repass.

But as in a grainfield one can sense the heart
wind-moulded on the circulating wheat;
yet cannot feel, possess, or see that part
– so I know how your breath and body meet.

THE PHOTOGRAPH

To energize the image of that moment,
the latent shine within your peaceful eyes,
I raise that copper tress, efface the skyline,
and as a bee might brush some paper flower
and delicately wish his work begun,
I take the air around your lips to mine;
sink back the brambles and the garden sun.

ON WORDS

Let us form our words in some October room
and let the meanings run, rounded and foretold
by the eyes' long glances, or quickenings
under white and gentle eyelids.

Let us form our words before the setting sun;
your corn hair grained with the wind;
your face trim and lovely, and the leaves
taken around us in an arch of emerald.

You, flushed as a woodman's daughter;
I, like some green giant down from the hills,
quoting the trees again.

ON AIR

Taking to your hands the torpedo blossoms,
the earth-buds and flowers of the dell,
you are the air's apostrophe, standing free;
the wind's daughter, holding to sky and sea
the miniature eternities of some holy giant
for them to possess in all their hearts' curl.

And when your warm shadow keeps the night away
from your quiet room, for you sitting there,
slowly but mightily, sweet from a century of stars,
god-like and grateful, he will cross your threshold,
leaving his golden breath between your walls
and passing all his bounty up your stairs..

ON LIGHT

It was of you I thought in the wind's following,
walking so much alone that the air went through me
and the chilled stones felt into my feet,
as I came to a lake sweetened with winter sun
reborn – a pillar of light racing and lovely,
cast in the waves' traces like god-wheat
spilled from the web of the morning's monotone:
it was you I needed to complete the wholeness.

When the goodness of light is seen by a wanderer,
then a god or his dearest friend should come for the witnessing
as he turns and shepherds his mind in simple boldness
to the church of his soul, and there takes together
near the hood of his bones those inward lights reacting
from the outer one – rebirths of some coarser stress.

I was of you I thought in the wind's following:
I could have told what pre-vernal hand drew a circle
around that water, of the beauty-land within.
Sacred by occupation of a pilot power,
secret with king-images, recessed and gentle,
I could have told only to you, this thing;
only to you – for one gracious hour.
It was you I needed to complete the wholeness.

NURSE, TEDDINGTON HOSPITAL

They taught her to cure, not by the cradled arm,
but by sharpness of heart in face of illness:
she learned the cheerful delicate trade of orders;
moving from bed to bed on the dull parquet,
bearing the attributes of the absolute
on the shoe of her poised leg.

Yet someone had given her glen talk,
taught her to enclose a sweetness in the husk of words;
to be an artiste before stroke-seared old men
until they felt within their map of bones
the keen warmth of a summer to come,
and knew for a chalice the small glass in their hands.

FLOWER-GIRL, ISLEWORTH HOSPITAL

Like a live signal,a poet should compress her
into a star-cluster in some constellation
for Shaw to admire. For this is another Eliza,
brash, honey-haired, a tawny thruster
straight-backed as a Roman fruit-girl,
with a skirt blue as the shouting sky.

Her hand of flowers, struck like a sensual torch
flares in rebellion at the gate.
In a sprat-faced house, rough with kindness,
on a hard bed, she will take her lover
with nine eyes and an open kiss
and a curse for all polite relatives.
She is a tawny thruster, this Eliza.

WOMAN IN THE TRAIN

I watched the summer waters of two eyes
so darkly mirrored in the window-pane;
not young, nor old, but tired tarns of memories
like deep grey lakes that could not flow away.

Across the faded seats I beamed a prayer
that the long transparent arms of angels
singing of high July and the Hesperides
would brush their pigments on a brighter canvas
to paint a holy healing riverway.

SESTINA FOR A FRIEND

A leather bandage for my twin-made eyes
is needed, so more fallow sight shall send
an image of yourself as image dies.
Then only these remain at senses' end
– the form you take as flower perfumes rise;
my finger's pulse; your sonnet word of friend.

So I may see and yet not see my friend
when space conceals the relics of my eyes:
for snow that drops upon the ground will end
deceipts of petals, not the saps which rise.
Within her head a candle-flame will send
a running light-girl, living when she dies.

Words and songs are made of sound that dies:
the thoughts that form them, living when they end,
will make in space a bride whose tresses rise
who follows silver turnings to a friend.
No need to hear; no need to use my eyes;
I know the hut of scriptures she will send.

Divide my arms about your hearth and send
between unheeded voices, shapes that rise
– sunshafts of feeling, heartfire from a friend
– a sense of warmth as flame of logwood dies,
until, as one, our shadows join and end,
born of a light I sense not with these eyes.

The playgods with their jack-hands made us rise
from mothers far in time: Earth's mutual friend
and circumstances shielded from our eyes;
they segregated tenancy, to send
to each that nuptial dream which only dies:
from their phosphor dark they watched it end.

But through ourselves this orphan time will end
when the clockwork of our breaths unwinds and dies
and all our senses separate, to send
no false diversions, playlights for our eyes.
My finger's pulse, your sonnet word of friend
will be exchanged for truth as mourners rise.

No manor hands, possessive, keep a friend,
but natural friendship means just common eyes
when common eyes sense Light and senses end.

ELAINE

Searching a shield at Astolat, one may find
an Elaine in the garden of the sun;
childless, yet in whose liquid mind,
soundless as dreams, the children run.

She has had her heroes, and her feet like sea-shells
caught on the deck of a daily beach,
feel the echoes of their steps across the ells,
though the waves of time have swept them out of reach.

Old and spinning by moonbeams, she will await
some sunlit grenadier through the trees,
like a rose at night whose mantic part was late
to time the perfume right for its release.

Place not your cheek on hers, or your earthly scheme
will rouse and fulfil but a part of her;
your image and your weir of words will seem
no knightly presence, but a talking mirror.

THEA

The glory of the moment in her russet hair,
Thea at the Eastern Stone, open to the lip of the wind:
love in her and before her like the cumbent rose
red and petal-thrilled outside the trilithons:
the glory of the druid about her
and coarse as rust now, the speech of Highgate,
forgotten in the purity of the circle.

JEAN

When the towers are new
and the easy moat is blue,
I will close your window, Jean,
and speak my love to you;
and in the western gloom
by the weary weaving loom
I will place my flowers, Jean,
like a living coloured plume.

When the towers lean
and the easy moat is green
I will open it for you
and watch your flowers, Jean,
to see the petals fall
and by unanswered call
will know your room has lost
the fairest of them all.

THE OBSERVER IN THE TRAIN

The minds are too conscious, the anticipation too clean and
    pointed;
the aims are neat programmes of events, not of the green and
    peeping,
rose-borne rites or the ripeness and decay in sowing,
and seasonal lamentation is well sublimated.
Happiness is restricted in the carriage, its thought force turning
all the correct curves between the ears, creeping
and drilled like the combed hair of a girl-child, plaited:
meditation is the act of not thinking:
the Quest and Direction are in the newspapers opening;
the retraction of the soul is complete, and dated
from the moment of sitting.

In that corner, knitting,
is one who came from the Void with the sons of men in her:
knowing her record, I have assembled her country,
named her Branwen of Britain, ridden the knightly
around her, sprinkled her stones with cool water.
Benedictions through island air, lightly,
and antique rays I have drawn from the daylight's bounty,
and eagles, posies, lights and precessions of tapers
in gliding ancient hands transparent with energy.
In the network wombs of the luggage rack, hidden and ghostly,
are veiled careful faces above this traveller:
these are the births of those she will meet with gently
in no bedroom dream, but sleep in reality,
with all colours and beauties.

These are my duties,
from the West, to take to her nightly, birds singing
and the brightness gone away from her hair;
from the East, amber, and a fine pale crown to wear
with a rose for her sun garment; bringing
the water of rivers, green bowers for prayer

81

from the North; wind-heather and saplings and fire
from the South, and the love of all men, stirring.
For who tells her now, on the hard and midnight stair,
of night-forces to gentle with, creating from air
arms with vulcan muscles, ripe and mellowing,
or brown and angled men beneath her sleep-high tower
all glanced and fresh from four-castle winds, and fair
– or of just one star seen sweet as a chapel light swinging?

ASHRAM

Thought was almost a wave-form,
an elusive violet
beamed from internal antennae;
western truths were without substance.

It was the way of non-violence;
the spirit was on their faces,
sun in their empty shoes,
the spinning-wheel ... a symbol.

PRAYER

In the season of snowbirds' return, a giant with southwind hair
abandoned strange eyes and despairing holiday laughter,
seeing a coral dawn powdered with golden starmow,
holy to pilgrim sights over the earl-glass water.

Far from the gala lanterns and holiday crowds,
seeking the presence behind the sky's ear,
he raised his great lands of arms to the caravan clouds
and prayed through the hands of his fishermen fathers
for a flame clean-wheeling a naked sea,
a god with a copper whip, a shooting star,
and the sound of the first blind oars of men
dipping in silence beyond the harbour bar.

HERB AND HOOLIGAN

Once briefly were petals divided and sprung
 - stamen-high stems light-shielded and flexed,
herculean cousins straddling wind,
green with maid and the son of a maid.

Skimming the hedges on crystal brooms,
the witches stole, with lanterns of gold,
making away on quick bent arms
with light-handed herb tokens...night-misted charms
to cast into woodlands, with black scarves flying,
in naked array, by pod and by stem.

Thief of life and lily-in-the-wind,
like a mad doctor probing, Winter pushed
thumbs in the keen dried lattice leaves.
Hands of bandit-ice edged with frost,
tight and slitting, split the stems:
frost-saw and hammer-gust ripped and tore them,
resisting like prayer-wires from their altars
of earth, root and humus, god-seed and bone.

ANTELOPE GIRL

Your copper hair grew slowly like coral
as rock-light awoke your body to glory
to walk one hip high through tropical nights
with eyes slanting wild harmony;
until, splitting the corn beneath the hot stars,
the beast in your long legs quivered
to mate unveiled with the giant heron.
Under the cusps of animal moons,
the brown face of your little fox-teacher
once turned to the white trees curled in vapour
to welcome the yellow daughter-panther
following from the slewed hilltop,
and your sleeping lips learned to lap
as you softly mouthed the low spring water.

But when the noon beaks of your bird companions
tilted through lost sunbeams,
lighting men telling of oak carts,
ripe roads and cities tall as fear,
you sprang away so quickly,
leaving only a closing river flower
racing in a small silver circle.

WARRIOR OF THE ICENIAN QUEEN

"This deeply felt and deeply moving poem is written with a hot head and a racing heart, and is as biassed as the Roman accounts; as biassed as it would have been had it indeed been written by a British warrior nearly two thousand years ago. Not only is it the history of the poet as opposed to the history of the historian; it is the history of the man actually involved in the events, too close to them to see any pattern. It catches fire and springs into life. It reads in fact, uncannily like the real thing."

ROSEMARY SUTCLIFF

WARRIOR OF THE ICENIAN QUEEN

The memories of an Icenian warrior who served in year 60 during the Boudiccan revolt against the Roman legions. (Passages in italics are the ghost voices of patriots from the life beyond.)

"The King is dead! ... The King is dead!
Prasutagus of the Icen
is dead!...is dead!"

I heard the cries, I remember,
putting sticks on the fire one rainy night
and kicking the ashes.

He left no son, and his weeping queen
placed his needs for the dark voyage
in the royal grave.

We had had enough of misery
at the hands of Ostorius
after Plautius returned to Rome;

the last light had darkened north of the Teme
for Caratac in Cambria with the men of the leek,
and we had no leader.

Our tribute was heavy and our mines were seized,
we were poor and had no lead to trade,
Our tribesmen beggars.

Then with craft, Seneca of Rome
had lent us ten million sesterces
with our buildings as bond:

a cunning act to chain us down
twice over to those who had robbed us
in the name of Claudius.

My brother, cleaner of the royal rooms,
told me in the shade of a roof
of the King's directions:

half of his treasure to his own Queen Voada;
half of his treasure to Nero of Rome
- to keep peace with the Emperor.

But like greedy foreigners, the officials of Rome
took no heed of the Icen death words
or the need for honour

and claimed undivided the King's hoard,
our dragon brooches of royal metal,
our tribal coins and our shields.

Sent by the State Commissioner,
the clerks and the counters, swaggering like owners,
listed our buildings and properties,

the money and mines in the lands of our fathers,
our carts and our ropes and our torcs of gold,
our timber, the sizes of rooms,

our wheels, our winter corn, our wood-poles,
our amber, our jet, our large pots
and our secret coloured glasses.

A road force of soldiery from the camp of the legion,
in a dust of death, with evil in their faces,
broke our night boundaries.

Eight men in armour took the Queen's daughters
for the pleasure of Romans (but one was our Marius,
so the gods were not absent);

others with madness and wine in their faces
stabbed our hunting dogs with glass
and cut the breasts of our girls.

Later we learned of the final treachery
when Seneca called for the sums of his loan
and ordered grievous additions.

This was the end, but the gods were with us,
our hearts clear of craft: ready for fighting
we had no reason for peace.

Acting with fury and mourning our plight,
we sent couriers of war down the long paths
to the green tribal spaces,

to the bright dominions of the eastern sea,
to the shore of the north and to southern men,
and to all who would follow.

I remembered when corn was taken in joy
through the hill gates of our royal city
the arms of our field women:

now they wept in the changing wind
with their hands to the sky where the gods were,
their tunics muddy and torn,

their High Queen whipped, the youth of her daughters
lost, their rooms emptied of treasure,
their sons bruised and flung against walls.

Where were they who once guarded the shields,
the brooches of amber, the holy lanterns
and the lead from the western mines;
who received the three-meaning messages
spoken from the land of the Dragon,
which were the wisdom and faith words?

There were noises and lights in houses of the Queen
as messengers from the great rooms
ordered the gathering of weapons,

and the rousing at nights of young men
to work in the wheelshops
of Tar-Annis the Thunderer.

Because of robbers and the men of the legions,
we buried our house goods
inside a bitter boundary

by sea-feel and tall rocks,
sealed with stones lowered on cradles
at five places which were not wondrous.

From other places we took arms
stored under grass lines near villages
in a range of pits known to our army.

Several had brought their house-poles,
sharpened and hardened in the fire,
shouldered like great lances;

many had the spears we issued
and iron killers of giant hooks
dangling on cauldron chains;

some carried shields and long knives
or had faith in their strong arms
like the magic of gods;

and others had just come to watch,
or, ready for prowling and stealing,
were there for the pickings.

But these were few, for our minds were heated
for the blood of Romans and the plight of our Queen,
and we were united.

There were chariots, so we kept to the roads,
and wagons with women and stores
that caught up at nightfall.

at first we sang together and slept
at darkness, then we moved by the moon
in separate armies.

To the middle forests we sent four tribal sections
handling knifers and spear throwers,
to wait for the Hispana legion;

to the west we sent spies through the fens
to find the paths the legion was travelling,
and the strength of its men;

to the Catuvellauni we sent fighters and stormers
with stores and provisions, to circle the camps
and starve men to weakness.

In the south I marched with my Red Queen
and a hundred thousand men of my island,
to destroy the Colonia.

Two Roman marches from my home earth
I met Mathe, daughter of Heng
the Marsh Dweller, who pulled me down;

but her eyes were wistful stars
that a man should not cover heavily,
and I was no luster under the Eagle

to lie under hedges with striplings,
but the son of my Icen father
who was kicked like a slave by the dogs of Catus.

So, like many, I kept to the marching path;
not searching the hut tracks for women,
but thinking of killing and Romans.

Do you remember the golden march of the Lost Voices
through the tunnel of the owl and the oak,
dropping down through a mine of singing land;
and the night forest breathing like a mother
over the wagons and the cooking-women
and the girls dipping cloaks in the streams
– when the leaves held that dark light
of evening, which carried the songs
of the battle-souls of our fathers,
and brought robins amd new men
and brown children, looking for Romans
from trees in the eastern morning?

Suddenly I saw the Trinovant men
shouting with war words and joy,
advancing on the side of the sun,

wanting our weapons and women,
too many torches, the use of axes,
and the sight of our Queen.

Raithan the red-haired
caught three stealing javelins and spears,
and knocked their heads against trees.

But many were wood families, simple people
run off their lands to make homesteads
and space for the foreigners from Rome

by orders of the leader Ostorius,
who sent his veteran killers
to live on their fathers' soil

and who dared to raise on the earth
which was Cunobelin's,
a city of settlers and a foreign colony.

I talked to many, we gave them cloaks
and some gold in exchange for milk
and baskets of watercress.

One, Brogdus, now fat for skirmishing,
was a freemarcher of the Wealden folk
who had fought as a youth in the marsh battles.

From seventeen summers before,
he remembered Caratac at the war-stream,
a true son of the Royal House,

holding a weapon of blood,
grim, on a high stone,
a carnyx bearer behind

– the advance levies of Gwydr
scattered over the wide corn
with the last of the coastal farmers.

Raithan the red-haired
caught three stealing javelins and spears,
and knocked their heads against trees.

But many were wood families, simple people
run off their lands to make homesteads
and space for the foreigners from Rome

by orders of the leader Ostorius,
who sent his veteran killers
to live on their fathers' soil

and who dared to raise on the earth
which was Cunobelin's,
a city of settlers and a foreign colony.

I talked to many, we gave them cloaks
and some gold in exchange for milk
and baskets of watercress.

One, Brogdus, now fat for skirmishing,
was a freemarcher of the Wealden folk
who had fought as a youth in the marsh battles.

From seventeen summers before,
he remembered Caratac at the war-stream,
a true son of the Royal House,

holding a weapon of blood,
grim, on a high stone,
a carnyx bearer behind

- the advance levies of Gwydr
scattered over the wide corn
with the last of the coastal farmers.

– the whitebeards, whose brown shanks
had once ridden the great horses
of the evening kingdoms

where the sons of Commius the king-warrior
had drunk mead to the memory of Vercingetorix
and the fighting over the waters.

Ay, we were all there under the trees,
awake for the last star-cloth of battle
– we, the faithful of the Island.

But many were the traitors in Calleva and Verulam,
the London colonia, and those with Cogi-Dubn,
where the waters were salt as his fish-belly.

In the dawn, we saw through the downland boughs,
wearing a linden leaf as a sign,
a fast rider from the middle country

who brought the good news of the killing of Romans
led by the legate of the Hispana legion
coming to aid the colonia:

two thousand men and wolfhounds in ambush
had caught the cohorts tired on the road
close to the camp at Calleva

and killed the whole company before it could reach it,
except for the legate and others on horses,
and the standard-bearer who escaped with the Eagle.

This was the day of the oppressed Icen;
the day of common people and blacksmiths;
the day of those with the long swords;
the day of the Red Queen and her daughters;
the day of Caratac and Casivellaun;

the day of Bear and Dragon.

In the darkness of many bush leaves
I left a young eye companion
who cleaned my armour and clothes

and took arms to a roadway from the colonia:
we saw no ramparts and no sentries posted;
we had time to encircle it boldly.

We heard panic noises but no shields glistened
from the Roman boar on the slopes above;
the day was ours like a prize.

Then we leaped in, yelling and slaying,
not like royal men, but animals
eager to rend their cagers.

Many were mad with fire and murder
and ran through the outer parts in disorder,
stabbing and clubbing old people.

Our women were worse, and gave every child
a death–blow. We were red–handed louts
– gone was our sense of rightness,

as if we remembered the day of death
when the Second hacked and cleaved our mothers
in the fortress near Durnovaria.

They were the captors of the leather tents;
they were the killers of all that moved;
they were the crimson-stained ones;
not those of Bran were their deeds;
not those of the brothers of Arianrod;
not those of patient Manawydan.

Then we saw armour on the temple steps;
they were only three hundred, but their shields were firm,
and they gave us some trouble.

Until night and through to the next day
at the high sun, we lost a thousand
before we divided them.

Soon we were through to their wives and the rest,
shrieking for life, but using axes
we soon made a silence.

And all we left to the air and the birds
with the evening sun on their fallen bodies,
as gifts to our war-gods.

Five times through the ribs they ordered the spears
– a god in their arms and they the hunters
of Roman meat on the clay floors;
sad, O sad, was the daytime of blood,
and the night has shadowed the sons and daughters
whose warmth has gone out of the house of the Roman.

But I and a few of my people paid tribute
to a man of valour who cut down a score
– a veteran strong as Heracles:

in the middle earth under his hearth
we lodged the old centurion,
a red fellow where we had finished him.

Then we found an old crone who told us of blood
colouring the sea near Camelot Dun,
seen as a portent of killing.

And how figures of bodies of Romans
were seen in the sand when the tide was low,
like corpses after a battle;

and how their Statue of Victory fell
as if it were true that the slaughter to come
from some foe would be found to be fatal.

It was surely the work of the forces of gods!
And so the country should hear of such things
we gave her a horse for her travels:

she and others stood for our kind
who would end the building of roads and statues
for our way of thinking in air.

And then I left, I had done with killing;
I had fought my best for my Queen,
and others would march to Verulam.

I remembered, as if it were yesterday
my father's mead yet untouched by the legions;
his house not trod by their feet:

as if it were yesterday, by the stones
where our druids met and talked of Jesus
to the many folk of my sister...

but more in my eyes were perhaps the grass
and the spread of the marsh-plants down the path
to Mathe, daughter of Heng...

This was the Island of the Mighty,
whether in the cold sunlight or the spinning breeze
or in the darkness over a river;
where the chariot-warriors were wrathful,
the ferry boats were plentiful,

where Arvirag was immortal;
where the great hosts of families
came armed in the light-starred downland suns
to the beaches new and southerly;
where the breast-plates shone with pride,
where the blue glass was elegant,
where the mirrors were bright as water,
and the birds flew like arrows of silver.

Who has relighted the Torch of Caratac?
Who has sprung from the Royal House?
Who has followed the Icen Queen?

Hers was the proud step on the chariot;
hers was the victory which was not a death;
hers was the blood which nourished the girl

whose peace was found at the heart of a Roman;
whose village faith was mingled with his;
whose child's issue was born to kindle

the lost Torch of Arvirag;
the druid's Sun for the son's Druid;
the One Light of Joseph's Church.

Now the valleys have known the uttered Word;
now the Torch has flamed in the winter sky;
now the beacon fire has charged the brands;
now the Hand of Hope bears the Water Sword.

COMMIUS

Commius of the Gallic Atrebates, an intrepid cavalryman, born near Arras (Nemetocenna), was created king of his tribe by Caesar after the latter had defeated it, as well as the Viromandui and the Nervii, at the battle of the Sambre during Caesar's bloody conquest of Gaul. Caesar subsequently used Commius's influence across the Channel to try to persuade the tribes there to trust Roman authority, prior to the Roman landings at Deal in 55 B.C., for which act of diplomacy Commius was imprisoned in Britain but eventually returned to Caesar.

When the great Gallic leader Vercingetorix led his massive revolt, Commius joined him and was part of the relief army which unsuccessfully attempted to raise the siege at Alesia, where Vercingetorix was trapped, subsequently captured and then ritually strangled at Rome. Commius then reorganised Gallic resistance, in alliance with Correus of the Bellovaci, which failed; he then turned brigand, intercepting Roman supplies, creating havoc, helped by dedicated friends. In about 50 B.C., he escaped from a Roman trap to kill him after a 'friendly' handshake, crossed to Britain and established himself as tribal king at Calleva (Silchester). His three sons later ruled over much of southern Britain. Elsewhere I have theorised that Commius was the Gallic king whose alliance with the Cordelia of Shakespeare's *King Lear* had some basis in earlier versions. Hence, the ninth verse from the end names his British wife as 'Kreidyla'. In some early tales, Cordelia's husband is named as Aganip, which is the shortened form of the name of a spring caused to issue on Mount Helicon by the hoof of Pegasus; according to Robert Graves it was also another name for Pegasus. The 'horse connection' is interesting as Commius was a highly skilled horseman. The first coins of Commius in Britain were developed from previous three-tailed mare patterns.

The poem is not history, but possible history, and describes a southerly march by Commius to storm Bibracte in 57 B.C., occupied by a traitor tribe, the Remi, loyal to Caesar.

E.R.

COMMIUS

Once we loved between the leaves,
my dear heart in her blue cloak
and I, hard-bodied victor of life,

laughing thrower of the light pole
by eye movements of sister and brother,
and lead horseman through the noon forest.

Our sky was proud like a face
over waters when I took sail,
fastest sea-runner of the tribe,

with hurling wind on the weathered hide
and the white strength of moon-cut wood
pressing joy to my feet.

Four hundred oxen at Nemetocenna,
two wives, three pots of gems
and a hundred strong wagons,

ten war-horses tethered
and the loving sun on my own corn
were my luxuries after my father's.

The rest was blood on my iron sword
often loosed from its fighting scabbard,
and my great coloured helmet

– my land and its grain swept of cattle robbers,
my warrior walls tall and strong,
my borders swelling with men;

and no man could steal my gold or sandals
but I took his head from his shoulders,
for treachery was my black hate.

I was a war man with comrades
clipped tight as a wide brooch
on the skin's own cloth

and my high words flew like arrows,
the callers of fierce and glad brothers
on the silver plains under the stars.

Like bright spears in peacetime
the women I turned had good thoughts
and lights in their open eyes,

except that night I camped by the waters
and some dark witch warmed my nesting flesh
under the village moon.

*

Sleeping or walking in the high green,
moving or looking five ways,
wrapped in my blanket breath,

I lived like a tall summer ox
until my tribe needed my arm
and my straightness of voice:

then I looked last on my silent hill-hut,
its skins on the floor in the hot noon sun,
and took up my helmet and spear:

it was time for the ox-hide of ancestors
to be found and wrapped round the living again
– the heart-clothes of the dead;

the grand facing armour of the inner warriors
who had sworn by the beacons and the young moon
in their warm once-lifetime walking

103

to close the paths of entry to foreigners
who brought javelins in the white peacetime
to redden the land of Berecyn.

Curving his sword like a mountain god
thrashing the rain from the sky with an ash tree
to clear the way for the sun,

my father had fought dark strangers
from the Suebi who blinded the gaze of the land
with rape and red battle blood.

By him and by Dis the Great Father
my body was spirit supported and held
by a sign as my high voice spoke –

"Sentries of northern hills and waters,
war-men of forts and commanders of ramparts –
like the voices of rain and wind

we came from beyond the Long River
and the paths of the land opened in peace
to our fathers' lost footfalls.

We, the Atrebatans, war-sons and sea-drifters,
travelling tribes of chieftains and fighters,
have moved under western stars

and struck our house-poles deep in the island
of bards; our brothers are wide, our children
suckled in Gaul and Britain.

Now the Roman crawls from the eastern hills,
drinkers of wine and stealers of honey,
to take and plunder our lands;

to make the tribes cowards and 'brothers' of Rome,
our men soft and peaceful – the slaves of Caesar
– our women like milk from a she-goat.

Comrades, a roof of brown hands calls
from the southern tracks as the shadows of metal
fall on the hills and the villages!

Gather your strength for the rock-grey roads
to Bibrax, your weapons like gods' swords
swinging, your heads sun-up and sweating,

until the blood's spirit leaps on the legions
and our watchfires flame to the mother moon
and the sky-clouds drop in hate!

Fight! Fight! Fight! Big cat and claw
will be yours as Galba's men, like tigers
in the reddened reeds of the crossing,

with the Morini, the Atuatuci,
the brave Bellovaci. Fight on the corn
of the sunland – to-morrow brings our friends!"

*

And so we marched like god-men
by the leaning light in the bent crag's eye,
by the bark on the long trees,

moving away from the home duns
with our eyes soft from women's cries
and the sound of our running children:

all the tribe's earth and the little voices
heard in the new summer suns
we would defend.

105

Ai! the long foot-beat of the stern house-men,
high heads raised in the country air
of the brown tribe-land:

theirs the keen shouts for the land of birth,
for the mothers and fathers of the youth homes
– the faces of colour

which rose in memory from the happy green
and the stone-wall guardians of custom lost
in the old home shade;

theirs the defence for the girls with the white teeth,
for the cooking women with the wide laps
under the trees;

for the great dog-friend of the hut group
left alone on the hill by the blue river
with a south-grey stare:

I would not cease to battle with those
who lit fires on the turf of the land of my fathers
and took animals from their fence-homes.

My lonely sun-face, as others,
rode like shining water-bronze
in the weald-sweeping rain:

sometimes at night I watched my warriors
half-sleeping on the steep rock paths
– all my strong friends,

and some who slept to dark night rhythms,
moving their sunned hands on their spears,
their fingers gliding

on shield-wood like man-sorrow
in its passage moving through patterns
on the cold shield-iron.

From the Long River to Samarobriva
there were two hundred thousand shields of followers
to check the poison of Rome,

and the fingers of warriors were firm
in the first light; like midnight horses
their hair streamed in the wind;

their mountain breaths warm in the mist
under the morning stars of ancestors
nesting in the open skylanes.

But I had a vision to put aside,
swung in the darkness of the sleeping night
– a black flower and grasses,

towering clouds and landstorms,
sheetheads of sky-axes,
a bird high-wailing

and a moon forest singing with dead men's bells,
my comrades with phantom spears
remote as water-branches,

and our sea routes blocked with dream galleys
launched from curving ghost harbours
in pale green waters.

After three sunsets we came to Bibrax
– a frowning circle of high-beaked walls
– a camp of dark traitors

peeping like mongrels through rampart gaps
- jack-faced, small crouching townsmen
whose minds were Caesar's

- the Remi! - weasels of loud noises
and pale hearts - crawlers of the forests,
patrollers of thin paths.

There was rain scent along the road
and in a grey space between mounds,
some crones smoked their fish,

as some thought to take food and rest,
with hard stones for tired eyes
on sleeping shoulders.

But most of us, moving like brothers,
hurled weapons from a dark ring of trees
- then took shields to the walls.

Five times we pulled earth and rock from below
until arrows and shots of stone, falling,
forced us away.

Then it was dark-time with torches lighted,
siege spears thrown from unseen heights
and screams of the dying.

There was death around in the vulture dark,
with mules, men, or man-gods moving
in and out of the yellow war lights;

and my voice was shuttered until I wished
the dawn spirits to warm the land
and guide all my battle placings.

There was a quarter of night to be run,
when a rustling against the south wall
put our hands to our knives.

I sent Madur the Red with fifty men
who travelled on grass like dark air, running
as silent as foxes.

In a ruin of stones they captured five Cretans
and took the bruised men at the ends of long knives
out of the evil structure.

In my tent of eight torches they laid them down,
with daggers at throat and a flame at their eyes,
with their ten bags of arrows.

Like a dog's were the sorrows in their opened eyes
but this was the breed when free and roaming
to mouth shallow hates;

so we kneaded their flesh across bone
to whip the airs of speech from their lungs,
flailing for truth-words.

Four talked and one remained silent
– the bravest;we made him a slave to clean weapons,
and the others we killed

after they told us with rolling eyes
they were Caesar's bowmen sent under darkness
to reinforce Bibrax.

Madur made a rush to the wall at dawn,
with Custen, Conn, Aillet and Mors
as rampart watchers:

in a mound of earth scooped from the side,
under a tree, they sat without alarm
raised by the Remi.

Hundreds of peering heads, loud words
of scorn, the hated Roman tongue,
the clash of metal

stole the relish from storming action
in the clean wind of day:
it was unsatisfactory.

The curse of the flaming fire from Conn
wavered then sang in his horn-bright eyes
and blew their minds white.

Then they returned with boxed hearts,
the moon-glow gone from their hair,
their faces heavy;

and Aillet the Young, of the Ox-Group
sank to his knees in the faint mountain light
fringing my tent.

I could tell the news, Caesar was here
in force, our southerly march too slow.
I turned to Divawc

to summon his druids – they scried the sands
but the signs were weak, with death symbols
and they were confused.

It was dawn; I sent for winemen and torches;
there were huts to burn outside the town
before we met Caesar.

I watched my men drinking, my firm heart hung
with inner flames; in a hard red clench
my war spear thrust.

Across a valley I saw some Nervii,
our northern comrades who had sent five villages,
gathered round tents.

I could not have known of the Sambre then,
or the blood and screams from my tribal brothers
fighting the legions.

We ravaged and burned and then lit war-fires
in sight of Caesar's hill and its trenches,
and got ready for battle.

                    *

The rest made history in my time:
the vainness of our attempts to storm;
the long return

to the waiting homes; the slaughter-retreat,
the re-forming, the final fighting;
Vercingetorix...

my dearest Kreidyla over the waters
and my royal huts in the softer glow
of wooded Calleva;

my great pride in my own sons
and all my tribal sisters and brothers
who crossed the waters.

Thus, it was all done, and somewhere
in the records it shall be put down.
But who will guess it all

when the white blossoms are on the trees
and the old blood faded under roads
of new men;

when April has done with Kreidyla
and her golden bowls are covered with berries
and hazel branches?

Who will guess it all in the summers
of those greater than I, Commius?
They will forget

the secret huts of the old kingdoms,
the sacred streams of the tribes' gods,
the great loves

by water and blood and mountain-ash tree.
But I ramble in age. Let us call it done
with kings and warriors,

pots of gems, fine war-horses.
Let us call it done - but who...
who will guess it all?

A SUN-RED MANTLE

SELECTIONS

THE SPIRIT OF THE GREEN LIGHT

Soft witch, abide and sing,
who lives by the inner and outer oak,
in the waters of life, the Nile,
and all holy rivers:

> with your green light held high, raise
> your maid-arm pointed,
> sing against blood-letting, be of love
> like those who drew water.

Soft witch, abide and sing
of the form printed upon the soul,
the thunder about the lightning,
the flesh on the spirit:

> with your green light held high, shine
> it on the hind and the white hart,
> and on all animals we cut to devour,
> which have faith but no tears in their eyes.

Soft witch, abide and sing
of Moses, Molmutius, Hu Gadarn,
of Ezra, Howel and Yesu,
dispensers of white glory:

> and with your green light held high, raise
> your maid-arm, pointed,
> sing against violence; until world's end time
> bless, and bless, and bless, the gentle races.

SINEWS OF STONE

By blue shepherds piping
below a looming cone of gods
I see the holy watersands
in white miles and lilies:

a stone girl of diorite
by moving lights and crystal hands
slants her pygmy moonland eyes
on steel trees breathing;

her doll blood has frozen
in play with lonely walking bones
and dances in the lighted tombs
of red marionettes:

astir, anthropoidal,
a green god from a flower land,
a swallow in his incense, moves,
his ox eye gleaming;

my throat laced with metal
I core his bull heart carefully,
feeling under double mail
by the bronze river crossing:

her queen head is bracing
to strain desire from cyclone cells;
she calls the water where I stand,
my owl heart beating:

her great face a tower,
I give her platinum and gold,
and near our jagged mated ore
a song wall is rising.

SLEEP

The night has grown with the stars
and, like the willow children
of the Catuvellauni
who rested their faces
in the moss and the silver bushes,
I too sleep, like a child of snow.

THE CHILDREN OF THE GIANT

Sea-master, sea-master,
of sapphire sand and dolphin,
and white random line,

are they quiet in your blue waves,
in the foam under the curlew,
or in softened blackbird snow,

or crying with lost eyes
in the black time,
the Children of the Giant?

THE HUNTER

Blessed the soul of the hunter, who cried in his poor bare throat,
seeing noon in a sky-net motionless over stones washed hollow,
and turned from his goat-horned gods, to kneel in a sea cave,
    strangely,
facing the new air whining from dripweed shores.

We were the awful circus, the pantomime riders
who came in their metal birds to the edge of the greenstone
and laughed under the plate of high noon,
when we found, clean by a kingpin rock, his knee-bones.

EUCIA THE BRITON GREETS THE DAWN

Was the cave sweet at the end, Eucia?
Come, naked-on-moss, little one,
white and marine, to the cirque of your father.

Rise from your cloak leaves and come, Eucia,
pilgrim-in-feet, tender and pinniform,
royal as ermine-with-light.

Caesar and Arthur, Guthrum and Ota,
will follow Hu of the Plains
and here some will build in great grey stone.

But this is the day you shall bathe by the rush-spikes
- those spearings-on-marsh, with the black fowl watching,
by nestings and wing-lift, and idle green.

Beware of the pit-man sheltering low
by ox-blood and wood ash and the teeth of foxes,
a skin on his evil rocks;

where the bark has gone from the long tree
and the blue wind sings through a heap of bones,
beware of he who pushes mud in the throats of children.

But kneel to drink with joy, at a distance,
then stand and cry like a god to the scarp-mist,
in high might - as your mother before,

with her grave-salt under your wet feet,
your small hands loving the clouds,
and that red christ disc rising......rising......

RIVER SPY, 54 B.C.

O naked river spy,
iron in your ringing voice,
watching a Dover bird hovering,
rising from your skins,
acting cocoon to the shy man
stroking his brown idol,
you have sent seven hundred black horses
plunging through the wide wheat,
their punishing hooves like thunderclouds;
surely the flesh of your wonder sisters
will walk in the fort of Cassivellaunus!

O naked river spy,
dauighter of the high sun,
we have driven the great stakes
into our white waters,
and we sit with our magic cups,
kneeling to the dark altar in the reeds;
we will take the hearts of a hundred Romans,
you have given us honey
and the yellow arms of our lamps
will touch gold to your hair;
surely you will sleep with men after the wine!

O naked river spy,
walking with the feet of light monkeys,
with the eyes of gods on our arrows,
as they come we will kill them
like jumping deer after the rain,
sinking the helmets of the metal strangers:
go, sleep on the moon-floor of our moor-hut
and hasten to clean your legs on the rushes;
your round sly face will see a tall man,
he will be as warm as a fox!

OUTSIDE THE ROMAN PALACE AT FISHBOURNE, A.D.75

Whose feet in careful sandals moved
past my oil lamp in the Palace?
My window eyes can see no shape
against the lights of the Western Wing:
a lover perhaps from the dark night
of the hidden waterways, where fires
of the People of the Kingdom
burn red with sticks – some Regni woman
pregnant under her brown cloak
claiming Maximus of the Guard.

The sea marsh smells of foreign dampness;
outside, their gods parade the mist:
we use their greensand and their clay,
their wood and iron, as peaceful builders:
but beyond the garden room I know
a century of tribal hands implores
a thunder-stone to break these walls.

CHURCHES LIKE STARS

Who stirs his limbs. who is returning
savage or saint, blooded from Viking
to the land of his father:
holy or hollow his sea-blue eyes;
coward or king in the vales;
remover or bearer of peace,
oppressor or friend of shepherd?
Savage or saint, coward or king,
who has suffered and languished
coiled like a dog at death,
chained beyond the Dee,
not for one year or two
but chained for twelve:
who stirs his limbs?
He, Gruffydd, father of Owen
and the queen-warrior Gwenliann,
 saint and not savage,
he, like Caractacus,
king and not coward,
good friend of shepherds,
valiant like Maxen,
in his eyes the blood of Mona;
he stirs his limbs.

He was protected by Lud's silver hand,
returning from the west to the land of his father;
for he stirs his limbs to build churches like stars
with the light on their walls.
All Gwynedd glitters with fondness,
and his eyes, sea-blue,
and the black of his kinsmen's
are as one.

LEO MYSTICUS

SELECTIONS

AGES UNTO AGES

White sing the living at evensong
where sounded the tones of the musical dead,
for the night stones bred the old high aura
which bounded the clerestory over their bed.

Heaven was where the old bards spoke,
hell the reflection of earth-green things;
waxen the faces where blood once flowed
- God's marionettes on artery strings.

Long was the sleep, but longer the learning
stretched where unfiltered moonlight wanes
for souls of the bodies of children and children
once under their mothers' counterpanes.

THE BETRAYAL OF ROSAMUND

Rosamund be her name,
auric hair-sheen
angelic in dawn-dream
before soldier's duty,
formed saintly rose
in extended image
moving polar to prayer
in his magnetic need.
gliding towards him
in gentle innocence.

Rosamund be her name,
advancing in creature trust
to this unguessed lover,
from field beyond field,
her hedgeline distances
a far reality, speaking
tone-high like bells
ringing silvered in mist,
treading dream lineals
through the sleeper's veil.

Rosamund be that name
now recognised, answered
in her love substance moving
through the mercuric cores
of the slumbering Earth-boy,
lips shaped to her beauty;
trust shattered, betrayed,
shocked to Gethsemane
as his young judas pupils
woke up and stared.

OCCULT HURRICANE

Earth's wild run is hag-blown on its wastes,
black-angel winds, trolling and patrolling,
power-bend tree-masts and the vegetation;

communication, continuous and telestic,
links to destroy high-green surface life
as if, with rain and storm, Orion's sword;

intrusive weapons spall the ploughman's fence
and where gold cursors spread and lead the finger,
riven splinters fly from every board;

oak ungrains its wood-soul to the blasts
as the potent shaft of god-iron strikes,
unfrocking bark, producing Typhon evil;

the pure thelemic chisel underscores
its will upon appearances of sense
and tourist atoms part before their Lord.

MAGICIAN AND MANIFESTATION

Fixed but alert, he meditated standing,
rooted in the transept of the structure
he had founded, closed in the astral dream
of a magician's moment, ghost nave behind
and all pews empty. His shaft of thought,
provided and ended with a crystal eye,
craned upward, scanning altar space, awaiting
essence of shape and archetype to form,
yang or yin, above the scarlet linen
bordered with silken cord and strewn with roses.

He had drawn his boundaries to repel all evil
in restless shadows or the falsely beautiful,
traced in each corner a cross within a circle,
designed four pentagrams shielding the quarters
against beast flank or sigillated demon;
he had called to Raphael, to Gabriel,
to Michael and to Uriel of the North,
ribboned himself with an oval of pure light
around his body's microcosm, placed mentally
before the altar a manifold of hangings
of veils of white figured with his devices..

Red candle, slowly opening gilded book
advanced their images beyond the veils;
fingered or clawed, two half-made holding limbs
materialised and grew, prepared the torso,
nakedly building from a zonal point,
tower-high, enspiralled with coloured energy,
the mineral facets of its giant face
in glinting amethyst, fire-laid phosphor
driven round empty orbits, chasing and rimming.
He bowed his head towards its planted feet.
When living rock with head of fate opposes,
if he looked up, death might be what it chooses.

127

CAVE LOVE

I shall walk to the girl-cave across the marsh
of the eastern water-birds, my torchflame
riding the earth of cold cousins,
to sit and talk by spices and iron.
Left on the western levels, my barley,
my staves, my great grey dog in the mist.

The arms of the Mother will shield ghostcallers
from our bride-night bodies until summer light.
When she hears the day songbird her eyes will take silver
from the blue-ring sky. I shall place in her hands
a sea-fish brooch and a spray of my land-flowers.

CORPSE

Uplever her night bones slowly,
expose them to lightning flash;
trowel her maid crystals gently,
under the burial ash.

Here clings her matrix mould,
worm-pierced, run with white root,
powder of blackwire hair
dry death on each living shoot.

The plough has revealed the message
of the faceless spine to the lark,
crushing her femurs, surrendered
as if to a ghost from the park.

BELTANE EVE

Through Hingston from Damnonian cave-holes
to points of assembly south of Sulis,
with chested heliotic symbols, shoulder stripes,
armed with Hathor quarter-moons, fun-horned dynasts
with brothers and sisters of the Leaf and Rock,
Eos-driven pilgrims, phosphor-faced ancients
(who would have thought the back-creaking ones
could have walked so far?), carts with cocks and costumes,
fur-strips, fair-weather moss to be held
against dawn winds for prophecy, girls
honey-lipped, young mothers in grace
with Iris, Flora and the returned Persephone.

    Not so much as a Zeus by your leave,
    he's too far off, his hand in affairs
    of all maidens and sea-nymphs,
    too many mountain-nymphs and probably
    twisting the locks of the long-haired one
    we fancied, cavorting by the grain-pit
    after wetting herself in the river
    - she'd the loveliest feet without sandals
    west of Horse-Pool Camp.

Then past the hill cleft where's evening sight
of the morrow's Pole of Hermes a stone's throw off;
let's eat and rest, it's free land, not king-grabbed.
Then at a moment the wolf-ring blackness
will split with the hundred-eye fires,
the sacred logs smoking and sparking, showing
shadows of people welded in the flames of El;
see like day, rowan and hawthorn blossom,
garland chains hung against the red-shot sky,
blue-flower faces in their gathered heaps,
the gentle shifting of cattle; here's wisdom
and heart-love for a fine New Year

as the Huntress keeps off the boars.

    Pleasure of Old Hornie
    watching the Honey-Isle,
    Alan of the Astral Light
    and Vulcan at his forge
    pausing to send his Maia.

so hurry or be cursed, here's no high silence
treading on Pryd's causeways
but the sounds of splayed feet, leaving behind
distances of small, bleeding pebbles,
eyes soon raised to the upper-vault stars,
to the Dog of Sirius, talisman of Cuno,
first-born male and barker-messenger,
announcer of the descent of Majesty.

    Leave the grey dog with the pots,
    old mothers with careful Hestia;
    bring your child-blood and renew,
    your grain is stored,
    bush-gaps soon repaired.
    Fail not the favours of the Gods;
    Ogmios. guard of the boundaries keeps ward
    and the druid Ynys has remained.

She'll descend to the Four Quarters and far out
to the passage waters of Anderida,
to the places of beacons. fire power, gorsedds,
assemblies, on this Day of Garlands.
Pole-dance to the Maiden. the Reviver,
who left six sisters in the day-sky
as this nymph of Atlas jewels our land.

    Even a litter for old Skin-Torn,
    who fell in the last weir, the boulders knew
    he wasn't fish. He'll come back

lucky from the May well, fresh-sprinkled;
the dawn hour's well waiting for,
what with the hands of the water girls
and the dose of barley and mint juice.
It's all worth waiting for; let's hope
there's a pin to drop in, to please Coventina.

GOD AND MAMMON

Into the book the images disperse
as publishers perform their Act of God.
In subsequent appraisal of the verse
the critics' heads may either shake or nod
and closest friends may even mouth a curse,
finding a phrase that strikes them as most odd.

And yet some oddnes is not really odd,
for associations in the brain disperse
in various modes. Some manifest a God,
a Devil or neuroses in their verse
- a resonance in thought promotes a nod,
and dissonance provokes a silent curse.

And so we should be wise to every curse
laid on our poetry, as not so odd.
To help sound nightly sleep to soon disperse
the nightmares caused when critics upstage God,
we hold the right to give the world our verse
though only close relations praise and nod.

And yet approval, causing heads to nod
can be a mental prison and a curse
when reality of life is judged as odd
if bodies burn and molecules disperse
- releasing other bodies before God.
Are sense impressions then the founts of verse?

The imagery which furbishes much verse
would hardly make the Angel Gabriel nod;
retailers of such observations curse
the mystic world as useless and just odd;
financial profits would decrease, disperse
if ledger headings bore the name of 'God'.

Some poetry can be inspired by God
in terms of soul's emancipated verse;
for atheists incarnate, a quiet nod
for progress on their Path may cause a curse,
and for poets finding 'higher powers' odd,
the chains of sense may break apart, disperse.

Let's fashion poems, conscious of His nod.
If we're reborn to write our human verse
our cyclic critic basically is God!

SEA GRAIL

Shadowed souls like doldrum sails
are sculpt unbillowed to the breeze;
bright the flag-hoist triumphs and even
the vessel-run with swollen canvas
lanced forward, surging to the light
– lateen energy bearing and prevailing,
taking selfhood to an ocean grail
– giant macro-symbol standing high
to moon, phosphorescent, love-lit,
set upon the cambric of the wave-foam
– sweet water-candle, Father of the Seven.

Here's navigator's solace
who in the making of his quest
took ship along the holy swan road
where, in gnosis or by testament
of history, supernals of the Spirit
repeat the signs perceived by prophets.
The best is on this sea-path, find
and sail it in the vessel of your innocence.

THE EXPERIMENT

This seven-part sequence is an attempt to see the human race as an experiment of the Creator. Attitudes, behaviour, events and comments encompass the phase of early man (ADVENT); man's conquest and rule (KINGDOMS); his wars (HILL 60); the make-up and quality of a nation (COMPONENTS OF THE NATION); material science in relation to transcendental considerations (SCIENTARY); continuance of a level of reality beyond death (GHOSTS OF THE QUATERNARY); and a return to the conception of the incarnated soul, advancement being gained by the attainment of spiritual consciousness (ARK).

E.R.

ADVENT

I

Cur and she-lynx prepared the advent
-apodal forms in rotting greenery
pausing in the foetid darkness
to lay their excrement upon a waypath
to clearings of a primal park
of forest tanglewood, or on the tracks
of virgin ox-roads of some future village
- an Eboracum turned in time from stakewood
stone, turfgrass. pounded earth;
or on the paths that old men,
praying to an unformed god, would follow
in tears and painfully to far green sanctuaries,
or leading where the thought was brave
to the dryness of a hermitage, set safe
by flying birds and ferns and pennyroyal
and Bridget-in-her-Bravery.
Spirit cannon in the blackthorn bursts muted blossom
- fire buds brooding in the pre-dawn
slate of silence, oppressed in witch-light
filtered from the white demanding moon.
A quicksword wilderness of hill-cleft ghosts
haunts secret places, until the dawn
dispels the demon in the floss.
Blood-ruby memories the tribal boy-kings,
now bone-white emperors in the ferment
of the earthbowl, hearthstones deserted.
Rock flatlands by leaf canopies warm pelts
of drying hare-skin stripped for morning sun;
crossriding pits and mounds in Urwald wastes
are barb-flung screens of old jack-brambles
- yet here, in some strange tinman's mist
is the evanescence and the forming phantom

of a half-gold, mystic, dreamlit Grail,
culled from its astral matrix as a symbol
to guide all quests in kingdoms to be born.

II

What early earth faith was perpetuated
in states of green, hand on tree-bole,
the simple touch of foot upon the ground?
What early child-forms moved the moments
near flower scent, in sunlight or in shadow,
or in the wind-high grasses where love-green
induced some potent auric chlorophyll
invisibly diffused in artery and organ –
conditioning raceguard for children to be born
in villages and cities. inside walls
containing blows and cruelty foreign to a tree
– a leaf-faith fading in the crocus memory?

This faith evolved in frosted fenlands,
companion to the sky for the dead and living
when hosts of souls from pinewood litter bodies
were resurrected to a parasol of stars,
to hunt again the mammoth and the bear
in the moonland of their calling Queen of Heaven.

III

Shuffling shadows of fire-fingers,
torchlit, scribing picture magic on stone pages;
caveborn children, naked, squatting,
watching the advent of wall-sacred art
eager on the limestone, wall-enshrined.
Rocklike forms of ibex, bison, bear
and bird-headed men in a mine of galleries;

shapes of wing, tusk, fur-form and fang,
antler, horn, mammoth, reindeer,
cave-lion and the Quaternary charger
caught in the memory of green-frame mornings
at Pech-Merle, Lascaux, Altimira,
Champs-Blanc and Les Combarelles.

What messages from canyon consciousness
twelve thousand years beside the shale?
What messages beyond moraines,
vertical toolmaker, primary hunter
and hominid of the riding flame?
Oracles, maze dances, ground-pits,
dene holes, burial mounds, shrines
denied, destroyed, the hearthwords silenced;
high life in evergreens exchanged
for concrete markets, cities;
lunar magic polarised to madness,
solar love reviled, except by hill-folk
- interglacial wonders, hut work, in museums -
Super-Ape, what messages?

IV

Wave tops like running diamonds
arise, break down, arise again.
The waters of dream bays of history
undulate with warrior pieces,
lost crested helms thrown up with flotsam
and the lifeless flanks of battle-horses.
Some life's recaptured on a Minster stone,
heraldic glass, still monument,
diapered shield, delight of blazoners,
charged ordinaries replacing death and pain;
saltweeds of time thicken like hair
blood-clotted from the axe and mace

swung to the target of some mother's son.
So Time' foetus ripens but to cut itself,
mother's magic destroyed by mother's magic;
cell-deeds programmed for a killing field;
the carnifex is urged to execute,
the blastula incarnate grows to slay.

The cargoes of red centuries are piled and sunk
in birthships unsignalled and unlighted:
gone to sea tombs every one.
The elements absorb, the land runs green,
the waters take, forget, obliterate.
What drowns in foster seas has ever gone
– fallen in the suffocating silt,
no memory of lost momentum
by bones picked clean on a fallow floor

V

Step light and kindly by the ancient barrows,
hillforts and earthworks. They had their sanctuaries,
their groves, horses under purple cloudset
of their once-day twilights; the shredded hours
of history fused in their greybird lands
of cavern, stone and woodflame, bear and bison.

You tread upon minutes of their gravebeds,
you of tissue media, dead fashion sheets
and vaporous words; their falcon underthoughts
have marked their distances, yet memories
still enter graven in your deepest dreams,
their potency diminished, but strong enough
to stir the archimandrite in your head.

VI

Earth-fainting but rising, returned to the light
through greenleaf arcadia, the gaunt elder guard
knew the first stories of the two-legged wanderers
by the scent of the firehills,in the air of the kingdoms.

By every late leaf of an old summer's autumn
there were always the children, in hope and glory,
always the children, rosettes of their days.

KINGDOMS

I

Here, in the high Andes,
for you, world tourist,
a certain physical innocence,
atomic purity lacing the blue air
around the peaks, footage
upthrust to fourteen thousand,
perhaps the same elementals sensed
in air, earth, water and sun-fire
which, being eternal, once brought
the eternity of repeated seasons
to the Empire of the Four Quarters
proud to cradle the light at Titicata,
the lake where the born Sun
burst in beauty over the Cordilleras.

Pizzaro, your dishonoured army
lusted for gold - the tears of the Sun
to those descended from Inti,
the God of the Sun. They came with madness
of white-faced devils from the outer sea,
discharging thunder and lightning from tubes;
they landed from boats with white wings,
carried strange crosses, wore close
a kind of grey stone which was unpierceable.

Pachacamac, who animates Earth,
Lord of Life and all sea-creatures,
did you forget the Conquistador-born,
whose terrible carpals. now lifeless,
once sinewed and bloodied, at Cuzco,
indicated the movements at chess
to your temple son, then cut off blue air,

silencing the royal Inca shout
- the garrotte in exchange for a room of gold?

Perhaps it is we, lesser men. who forget,
for later you gave your holy sign,
quaking the old temple foundations
into the sight of honourable people,
breaking covering convent and crosses
to display the stones of his rightful home,
the Golden Temple of the Empire,
in repeated season.

II

A kingdom for Blue-Beads.
ankles adorned,
throne-room with lion cubs,
leopards and cow skins
for the royal of Royal Toro.

Rukiidi, Caswallon
before the war-Caesars,
before the Amins,
before the Obotes
-once sacred your huts.

Empagno proclaimed
your noble possessions,
your gracious high ancestors.
East of Moon Mountains
let all your fair women
be named Engagu!

III

Cortes, like Francesco Pizzaro,
does your historical conquest lie
judged by "an aspect of eternity"
beyond all ultimate good or evil?

Herman, you trampled on rank without class,
democracy balanced between day and night
in the rhythm of corn growth, water and sun.

Cleopatra wore emeralds - these were your symbols.
With your horses, steel armour, new gods,
you commandeered all from the innocent Aztec
who built Tenochtitlan, the world's richest city.
You accepted honours and the plumed head-dress
feigning the demiurge Quetzalcoatl
come from the east in the Year of Ce-Acatal.

On the Day of Saint Hippolytus,
that one who was destroyed by horses,
like man-horse amuck you mocked your religion,
destroyed the City of the Great Salt Lake
In the stench of a thousand fires,
by your savage distorted values,
your Spaniard was pagan; that Aztec the saint.

IV

Marye, thou took for sovereign lord
thy king, knew of His Grace's word
as law, were obedient in his sight
as trusting daughter; reason and right

were all thy father's; suffered thee
his will that made a bastardy

144

of thy mother's babe; knew her true bride
a second time; had better died
than see that Catherine beguiled
by Anne he lusted on for child.

Remember the lost Dauphin, thou who
wished for naught at age of two
of state engagements for the price
of power. Then Elizabeth; then at trice
Edward found as his bearer lost
this life.

He thou loved great at cost
of inner faith, God's grace to brother
gave who reigned instead; another
stop to thy mind which knew they axed
the Lady Salisbury.

Set in grim mould at youth, thou wept
comfortless – all friends swept
head from body. So went away
all links – Poles, Courtenay
and others.

Still there remained one
thou'd chance a doubting kingdom on
– cherished Spaniard who when wed
deigned no travel to thy bed
before thy death, clasping a phantom,
that swelling which would never come
to foetus.

He thy wrenched body bid by proxy
to name as heir Elizabeth, yet hid
consuming interest to espouse her. State
enfired thine own person, inburned a hate.

Good Catherine, now in spirit come ye
to the soul of that Marye still called bloodye;
forsake thy bones, Peterborough laid.
Come, comfort thou, thine own poor maid.

HILL 60

I

In the summer month
Julius, as they named it,
cliff-watcher, tribesman,
one with Caswallon
great son of Beli,
sheers down the day
his pinnacle gaze
to eight-hundred decks
of Imperial ambition
in the slow coastal swell
with Caesar's five legions
helm-aimed for Prydain
north of the Trinovant
from Itius of Gallia.

Who should oppose him
where sea gods have failed;
who should then challenge
this king of the war-run
from Rhodanus to Liger
past Sabis to Mosa?
Who sails to your island,
the haven of Albion,
with Apollo assurance
but a foul executioner
of Suebi. Treveri,
Bellovaci. Carnutes?

From the rock of your scorn,
old man of the cliff,
thunder your spear
on the turf of your homeland,

each counting, each striking,
one less to return.
No cursing legions,
no hillfort besiegers,
no men of Bellona,
no killers of Caesar's
shall trample your corn.

II

Bear-Folk Chief Arth-wyr,
coiten Ar'wyrauc his stone,
chased the Twrch Trwyth,
spine-glittering hog,
southway to Kernow
across Carn Cavall.

Hog warriors of Plautius
embarked from Gesori,
rough-riding wavelanes
in Fretum Gallicum
to Kantion coastlines,
or, westered in currents,
landed at Bosham,
south of Caer Guinnion,
hog-weapons bristling
in the sun of Caratac
(the light of his father)
and Gwydr, half-brother
- king-elder from Cuno.

Then some with Vespasian
from the Second Augusta
went to hillfort Mai-dun,
armed with stone engines,
hurling brain-biters;

before then to Vectis,
four-cornered diamond
and Isle of the Joyous.

The Twentieth Valeria
and hardened Fourteenth,
the tusks of the hog,
ripped Mona's neophytes
with spathae of blood.
Hear now the star-cry
of priest pierced with pilum.
The long undernight
of Deceangli dawn
was mournful with weeping
when the red-fever sun
lighted the hog-blades
bloody with druid.

Somewhere the leavings
of the fated Pannonian;
somewhere the blood
of the old Rhine legion;
somewhere the Ninth
in rusted centuries;
somewhere the aggers
of those murderous Aprils.

III

and you
once the travelling man
mi roger
gone to the colours
yet thru tears
you brush mi parlour cheek
in wisps each year

on that november day
of cart and fog

our vows taken
in whipcorn summer
the running sunbars
riding hedgetops
and stook angels
in orange glory
betrayed

i still believed
you were not there
mi roger

not in that khaki
in the long box
on the rocking cart
not you returning
on that day
bloody cloth
torn open
emptied of
our summer love

IV

In outdoor grey, before breakfast,
Farmer Boromée was fencing his cows,
French blood in its rightful place,
coursing veins, as he hammered the pickets
for securing the chains, on the Thiepval Ridge.

Le sergent, enemies in his eyes,
seeing guns on every oak branch,
acorns, pine cones as lumps of shrapnel,

sheep droppings as powder trains,
alien barbed wire on every post,
gave orders to fire a volley.
Every vacuum was filling with Hun,
no chateau was safe, and now at Authuille
La Comptesse had fled from Thiepval.
They were quick, these devils from Mons,
advancing through Picardy.

Down in the village, the hens fed,
his wife, efficient with the chores,
had coffee simmering on the farm stove,
moved bright as the new day.
She could not know the thirst for coffee, of life,
was over, her man spread bleeding,
hammer in hand, at the base of a cow picket,
shot as a German erecting a barricade.

V

New son of the nation,
you will forget your brave young grandfather,
God under his duckboards at Passchendaele,
his unrecorded prayers barren in Flanders;
forget the Hindenberg Line, the Arras advances,
the bloodied trenches – the cry "stretcher bearer!",
the mines at Messines, the Lewis gunners.
Superior thoughts, not those of old men
who balk your rave path like dithering fools,
will rule your thin temper towards the 'Contemptibles',
for those at Armentieres who rode for Allenby,
as you storm from late-night discos
in your green Cortina Mark 3.

When you cross the Channel, with your luncheon pack,
strolling in freedom down Paris avenues,

151

will awareness in your brain, that organ
grooved with your heroes – Kojak, Cannon and Clint,
enphase the glint of bayonets at Verdun?
Throwing your coke can away in some field,
will you remember, broken by bullets at Louvement,
Theuriet of the 85th, with cigar and swaggerstick,
forsaking life in the same time of movement?
Will the back of your bright eye see fallen French
at Herbebois, at Chambrette, on Hill 344,
when their fate was arithmetic – one unit of glory
five units of stench of their opened bodies?
Here lay the embryos grown from the 1890s
whose mothers graced days at Chantilly,
Paris, Beauvais, Lille and Auxerre.
Will you place lilacs on their garden seasons
– for Pétain's two hundred thousand, who knew
his " *Tenez ferme! J'ai confiance en vous!* " ?

What of candles guttering, whispers on the breaths
of the very old very young, whose loves went weeping?
..of that tavern doorway, third at Framerville,
repaired by Jean Renet, who planted flowers
beside the cobblestones, made in that France
of yesterday, splintered by a seventy–seven
not far from that fated summer cornfield
where Mariella watched in innocence
the black–crossed Heinkel circle above the spire
of Our Lady's church, whose guns spat harm?
What of the lock of golden hair
curled in the tunic of the pilot Hun –
and why should the flyer cherish that one,
yet kill the other in an accident of death?

VI

Do the new weapon-makers respond to the cries
of frost-hardened warriors, who missed the Green Lady
but rest in the groves of the Mighty One?

Do the guided missiles sweep the air-paths
between star-temples of ancient priests
and the linking star-shield of the eternal cosmos?

Does the bull in the sky at the sign of Taurus
still oblige watchers to pray for fertility
in the management of short-horned cattle?

When they meander among the flint refuse,
do the ghosts of Tardenosian hutwives
disturb the cutlers of Wincobank Hill?

Do the carriers of men on the motorways
follow the great British chariot lanes
which were cut from primeval tanglewood?

Is the admonishing finger a trigger-digit?
Is the angry arm now bearing a rifle?
Does the arrow-pull muscle now push a death-button?

Do the shade-men of Queen Victoria's Rifles
remember the killing in taking Hill 60,
the mud of craters, the hissing of Very lights?

Did the air-raid sirens of modern Lutetia
oversound the carnyx of the Bellovaci,
oversounded by blasts of the Strombus horn?

COMPONENTS OF THE NATION

I

Framed bloodflow, kinetic illusion,
drifts tribally, includes graded cells
of functional significance, leads to
travel in naves of initiation, each time
starting with baptism, chosen life-womb,
enwalling a forgetting, a parting
with occupied levels, transmuting
to world-naked soul, karma shouldered.

That ultimate stardust is attained
by severance with links to severe beauty
incapable of being entered
until the re-promising wheelturns
course the dark night of the soul,
last time to a purpose, opening
to a divide, perilously misted,
filtering a gorgeousness, jumped
by no hurtling mare disturbed
by flank-whip or goad
disguised as final instrument.
Wings grow, strengthened,
the mane loses its coloured tossing,
whitening to disappearance,
faster than known light.

Until then, await no cloister
for filling the silent heart;
the thrust is tribal,
national testing grounds
with tools of corpuscles, cells,
nerve messages, movements
where harvests of wheat, barley,

154

have an innocence.
Where there are offerings
will be the rejoicing.

II

In the unity of the Kingdom,
Alfred protected the mode,
be come his memory,
thrice blessed.
Candles in lanterns lifted in wind
are never extinguished;
arrows to an Edmund,
burning of books, monasteries
are unifiers against shire breakers;
in shield wall against raven
is the war-grouped nation;
in the song against evil
is the questing nation.

The mode of the church
is commonly placed to sustain
against fall from grace, to yield
a kindred in soul, but attempting,
maintaining without knowledge,
sustaining without progression,
training with inadequate tools
of prayers and hymns, rote words.
This is the general mode
of the church of the nation,
Mūlādhāra for masses,
flocking at the four-petalled lotus.

III

The mode of a kingdom is stabilized,
established by right outer thinking;
feudal flowering by a good lord
creates steady history.
The squire conveys a bounty of substance;
the knights their truth-fight, chivalry;
the merchants offer their goods;
Imperial life flows through the affairs
of grooms and chandlers,
kitchen-maids, poets, ushers,
stewards, gamekepers, blacksmiths,
generals, goodwives, yeomen,
apothecaries, sheriffs, archers,
farmers and farriers. This is the mode
of the Kingdom of a nation.

This is the breaking of a Kingdom:
sensitive factions replacing basic belief;
unrighteous control of prerogatives
of thegns, goldsmiths, masons, husbandmen;
replacement of limits of traditional freedoms
by unrestricted freedoms of fashions
entered into, promoted by, those
for their own use, or the use of groups
for their own satisfaction, impoverished
in knowledge of time scale
or uncaring in attitude;
the flouting of laws of copyright;
indulgence in criminal activities;
the lack of respect for ancestors;
vulgar distortion of the language
and avoidance of places of worship.

Let the Flag be prized.

IV

Cavalry squadrons are tribal,
drilling, wheeling, cantering,
whether the Greys or the Inniskillings
– a central reminder of debts
to the Fallen, stable progression
of Kingdom, protection of monarch,
described in movement and ritual,
processionals, funerals, guard-mounting,
statues of Those Who Served, national causes,
observance of royal occasions.
These are the bases of Kingdom
and patterns of nation within.

V

Tunnels of history have swallowed the passings:
of light at the end we rely on seers and soothsayers
who divine with the blue wire of communication.
Spirits call in the void, men of old battlefields,
caught in magnetic memory, re-enact wars,
playback copymen, ether-suspended
for those who will see, shells of the past
hollow with hollow particles, returned as if solid.
Above the long ghostline of latitude forty
are the redcoat voices of Salamanca, Talavera,
the salt-throated shouts of Trafalgar, St.Vincent;
time-remote bird flights over Granada;
dummy-caught over Albion - Newton and Nelson,
oak-servants Browne, Langland and Spenser
and all flag-variants.

In the five-sense world
is recorded the loss of Frederica's silk handkerchief
by some microprints set in the clay;

Dee in the shift soil moves slowly through Mortlake,
his Tudor molecules gone up to Kew
– his ears, now chemical units,
which canalled the voice of Gerardus,
have travelled to Cumberland's garden soil
along the drains.

These are the hidden components of nation:
invisible heritage blending with heritage
of pictures, books, deeds, tales of old heroes;
myth outlasting chatter of the age,
murk of media, press–line erotics,
products of disordered minds, vulgarities
of sex–driven writers of unbalanced boundaries,
the posing of fashions by art institutions
supporting the time–driven present,
always tracking the running rabbit
without heeding manifestations
of that which is true and permanent,
outlasting all.

VI

Everyman from noman form uses tribe or nation,
discards to void paragon criteria, sorrow,
vitalities of morals, linking obligations;
extracts pabulum for record, homes to furrow,
leaving to native field the fossil parts;
remakes for acting; in new wig and gown
takes station for the morrow,
component with a steelheart store
inbuilt from seed, pure light denied:
the platform names and loses to another
– hearts have no name.

SCIENTARY

I

After Newton and the apple-fall,
alchemy of soul was something east
of Delhi; all-seeing and all-knowing
the probes of sensor, telescope and radio;
mammals of skill made chemical advances
and found the carbon godhead,
coal, graphite, holy diamond,
useful for heating bodies of the faithful,
writing in pencil selections of the Word,
entries to the corridors of power
– a modern three-in-one; not what they were,
fire-elves and spirits of the wind.
Foetuses inbuilt with five-sense birthrights,
although of levels close to early beasts,
grew imprinted with cerebral links
useful in situations of the faith,
detection of incense, touch of Christian handshake,
taste of communion wine, sounds of bells,
reverberating gongs, the sight of spires.
Mankind was raised one Jacob's-ladder step
above the simian, the laser beam
allowing life to clockwork genesis,
but consciousness of soul in standing station
of blood and bone and cells and body fluids,
moment's devices, although determinants of karma,
neglected or misunderstood.

II

Neanderthals in brokers' cavelands
finger the keys of fast computers;

control of nervous processes and functions
reducing havoc in the growing jungle
of cerebral branching and the mixing blood
– patterns of astral search soon lost
behind the exoteric imposition
of fashion, business morals, new cultures,
advertisement of wants and not of needs.

Though organic molecules, arrange, mature,
and blood and lymph are formally entrained,
life is not the running or the walking,
colour of the skin or heart–pump working,
movement of fanatic tongue in talking,
or body–framing skeleton performing.

There are those who breathe strange oxygen
– those homotypes who passed behind the veil,
remembered once for skin–imprinted kiss
or visits and revisits from a friend,
now pathway pilgrims to supernal suns.
Somewhere perhaps is Einstein in his grace,
who said the Lord was subtle, not malicious,
ensouled and guiding new Aquarian schemes,
vibrating rubrics into curving space.

III

Outwingers on the floating lace of time,
men and women, once corpses in Castilo,
deep in the fire–hills of Cantabrica,
elsewhere west and east, victims, conquerors,
now molecules of broken bones,
relive their energies in perpetuity.
The fabric record of their deeds in history
stays phantom in its ghostly Mechlin finery,
re–formed, alive, in pseudo–solid,

land-locked performances and exits shaped.

In timelessness the Ace of Paris flies
behind the cowling of his blood-red Nieuport;
within Navarre, Bruchmuller's batteries
define Bethune - a wing of Meteors
continually surveys the Mall.
Space remains, action still proceeds.
Once more the riding knights of Charlemagne
spur horses, but through office walls;
the blood of battles stains a thousand car-parks;
astral fiddlers and right holy friars
disport in gardens while the washing dries;
and still the Asgard casters of the runes
scatter their futhorks in the alien halls
of Woolworths, Marks, Fine Fare and C & A.

IV

Angelic dynamite, the Countenance
knows the human allotrope, the changeling
transmuted from some evening dinosaur;
knows all vectors of the space in Malkuth,
translations of geometry and herd,
all land and liquid masks of moving planets,
lovers, calculators, dreamers
who perform their cycle on the Wheel
and pass or pass-not in their ambience,
progress sweet with nectar lanes
or paths in dereliction, dry
- mundane sight of marginal reality
eccentric to the centre-fold, the vista.

V

Nature, in the sum of things,
sets no limits to left or right,
compelling body to be an end of void
and void the end of body: in this light,
Lucretius, ignorant of Black Holes,
believed void and matter were infinite
– for if bodies were absent on one side of space,
that side would be the gate of death, and flight
of all matter would occur through it.
But for separation of bones, without choice,
by a time gap of reactive particles
on a sixteen million hour engagement,
the cells of his right metacarpals
could have closed on those of Wheeler or Hawking,
and frequencies structured on breath, called 'voice',
might have mentioned the oversight, that roles
of gates of death and infinity were not incompatible.

God was still latent during use of gunpowder,
prayers before blasts were not unusual,
assuming He would guide in His wisdom
all cannon balls leaving the source of petition
and divert those approaching it.
But when $E = mc^2$ triggered the Bomb,
a Saviour's Day was subject to question:
divine predilection, indeed, was tantamount
to admission of faults in the system
–wisdom was better replaced by prophecy.
Gravitational collapse, the tomb of the Easter Jesus,
cosmic law – still need to be reconciled.
Our favoured traditions around entrance and exit
of our cellular lives will need revision.

GHOSTS OF THE QUATERNARY

I

Somewhere in Brigantia they move through hosting flesh,
quiet ears perceive; drones of shuttered silence
in-skirl headbones, penetrate post-infant sutures,
molecularly incomplete; auras mingle with the hosts.
They pass where pass not form or frondage,
through cottage, house or church, below a mound
or churchyard grave, following real dreams;
shell-linking with your shell, they show their world
to you, veiled in sleep's pit, share remorseless deeds
expiated only by a green man's law.
Their sins and yours are fashioned under stars
where fly the deadman's owls, or in whiteworm tunnels
where bright is evil and the path-thin ribbons
in the red rock hide nothing time forgot,
but creatures which *you* made, remembered
in the likeness of your thoughts. Take eye in dream
of gibbon-haired ones, shoulder to shoulder
in smoking caves – the only birth they knew
was from the opened dark of thought wombs
which bred them from obscenities.

Pale wafers on the mind-tree,
unborn phantoms pulse to birth;
membranes shiver, filled with energy
of thought, purity or impurity,
paradise or slum, designed and toned
from loving moments or grenade trajectory.

You sing, you are the song; you think, you make
and bind these flag-toys to the cosmic network;
Brigantia's dreamblood fills those stalking ghosts
which talk and move in caverns of your mind.

II

Neuroscientists admit no phantom presences,
the brain is its own computer; consciousness
is correlated with nervous activity;
horizontal movements of the neck of a barn owl
are stimulated by time differences of sounds
generated inside or outside barns, arriving at the ears
to give cochlear signals to midbrain neurons;
vertical movements of the neck of a barn owl
are also stimulated by time differences of sounds
between ears, because God gave the barn owl
one ear higher than the other,
and the midbrain neurons work it all out.
Which explains why owls avoid Parkinson's
by getting away from it all.

Neuroscientists admit no God
or ghostly agents. Good or Bad does not floor them;
valuations of systems are good or bad
if they do or do not promote satisfaction
or aid, or assist self-maintenance.

Neither can one see supernatural visions,
for they are absent from ocular attention
and cannot image behind organic lenses
which collect signals by successive jumps
in recognition of objects of interest.
In any case, perception is determined
by what is already there in the brainhouse,
which is fully leased out, with no room for God.
There is always the Road to Damascus
but failure to receive an immediate reward
for the replay of a past emotive image
would act as a negative stimulus
and result in happenings being unreported
as irrelevant to self-maintenance.

III

And what of you, Celt of the time-run,
when you pointed your arm to the high sun
and made the sign of your god?
Renewal of life by ghosts was a tale
to be taught to children – when the sweets of the dead
were buried with the dead, chained talisman
below the head, war-belt near,
coloured dish with meat from the chase,
grey hunting dog in the south pit,
stallion, still and golden, by the thighs
– on a square bark sheet, a long line for fish.
Uncovered by new strangers, the body dross
– unseeing a new guise and level,
ghost and possessions, in counterpart reality.

IV

Still then ghost-fable older than Jesus
when Merlin of the Isle of Bardsey,
banished emanation fragment,
once-enchanted image of higher consciousness,
revealer of dragons in Wales,
counsellor of Arthur, in glass imprisonment,
sensing midstream humans, re-formed
on astral levels for the good of the Kingdom.

He knew of the left-handed paths, killing fields
seeded in morrigan darkness
– the old dispensation had escaped from vipers,
iron traps, spells of untrained wizards,
enchantresses – but the creatures of groves and rocks,
elementals, tree-spirits, were reduced,
shadows of Mammon obscured the sun-soul
– just in time before the horn-notes would be heard

165

and a new Balin deliver a blow so dolorous
that fields would wither, re-scar
- all his good work undone for ever.
Also, the shields were down,
the lances closeted and lost,
Igraine's son long unfleshed,
the four elements insufficient in seasons
of lost consciousness – alchemical dances of atoms
changed to war-tangos of dangerous energy.
And the Table of Third Importance,
after Christ's and Joseph's, which was Uther's,
had been stolen or put aside.

There was a Grail still, symbol of greater symbol
- the Corbenic, and Merlin was its Mercurius.
He would use the Reviver, urge a new Galahad,
re-fruit, in the eye of light, the wilderness
of these trafficking aliens, bring new values,
secure his land for another two thousand years.

<h2 style="text-align:center">V</h2>

Where are the bones of Morfa Rhiannedd,
the bones of Helig son of Glanoc,
the lost cantrev of Wales,
the echoes of the island feet of Joseph?
Man and Quaternary elk
are lost with the sand and the star-grass;
like waterfall ghosts,
dwellers by meres and hamlets
have gone with the white fox,
with the black forest oaks by the Mersey Bar
- Singleton Thorpe, Tarleton Moss, Marton,
Ince Marshes, Barton, Simonswood,
all buried with herdsmen's huts,
with Agarmeols, Aynesdale, Gripnottes,

Butterclinning, Waingate and Atefield
- Ravenskills, Selefures, Greendale,
Romsdale, Melcanrehow, and all to seaward.

All ghosts in the old oak,
or as faces in meadow rain,
they linger, forest familiars glancing
between long boughs crossed in the wind,
sun on their firewatcher faces,
thinned edge-lights, disappearing, reappearing
- high phantoms of continuums, of dogdays
of star-run seasons, playmates of blue herb time
when upland bodies climbed and walked.

Now but moving eyebirds, fragment souls, like Sholen.
Shell-memory wishes her to speak again,
to see that sister-head by briar paths,
to touch lips known by salt-moss
when we shared a waking warmth
on our land below the birds.

VI

Speak again, dear love,
thread out from grey-dawn moor
to meet my pilgrim fragment;
cold chapels in your eyes,
remember with hosting breath
that you were Sholen
who once filled water-vessels;
that our cheeks, wet with rainwind
once sang of life and glory,
of old land-pipers
bone-twisted in their Caledon
who marched with battle-leathers swinging
to fight for their mimosa lands;

remember how we pledged with foxes
our misted secrets in the northern ground;
how the horn-notes of the Bear
disturbed your cousin's flocks?

Now countess of a fairer wind,
will echo mock the memory,
when, sweeter than a westlight rose,
as evening bride, by scent of lilac
and the sleeping berry, you drew
your cloth of holy apricot aside?
- dear one-white-pearl, will you recall
our nights below the dragon star?

Come, meet my spirit, light in life-green
your heartface and your folk-lips;
turn towards my evening grey dog
long buried by the Wall.

Nine paces onwards point your arm
where rest my broken sunken bones
- go, whisper to their crystals
they once made love to Sholen by the rowan tree!

ARK

I

Surging woodpower or the greenheart force
ancient as the hills, stays wound or rested
under playgrounds, shops, synthetic areas,
the passages and paths of new boxed towns.
The paupered urban spaces, walled and soulless
are cruel with concrete car-pits, paving, subways,
form gaolers' roofs above; bedrock below
completes the prison sandwich, hard compressed.
But born again, some Sherwood Marians still
step disco in the smallweed borderlands,
unleashing token turnings with the brilliance
of foot and folk-eye blended in blood memory
of years of scented boughs, the fertile sense,
tree-love and sun-dawn singing of an age
when the ark of consciousness was in the bower.
Meadows in the mind recall the calling
of friends in season, hamlets and their fields,
though authority works dazed with natural crimes,
seed chaos spread by every tool and tread.
Did Peter's Rome bleed out green pagan love
behind a metaphor of crucifixes?

II

Iron-frost days,
hours of leaves falling
at calendar's end,
weather cycles,
sweet-scented months
for berry-picking
have touchable moments

seen and sensuous.

Unseen, inviolate,
essence of ark,
as birth invader,
pervades the grossness
of wide macrostructures
of stranger cells
-compound replacements
of forgotten dust,
fallen in mould
or consumed by fire.

Flesh issues
at womb point,
incarcerates consciousness
for the lifetime;
the inner Christ
rebonded for its freedom,
learning to ignore
monstrance of symbol
in the Outer.

In time's gallow seas
the fish swim shallow,
silt piles, envelopes
a million Edens;
a thimble of faith,
a pittance of psalms
lost in eternity,
a Saviour's arms
historicity.

III

Prepare, Evadne, for your chieftain's death,
the practice of your widowing
or a natural parting from your nesting.
Whether by Zeus at Thebes, light of fate
from war-stars, tremors, floods, old age,
the feather flight of soul to Kether state
surpasses three dimensions;
Descartian muliples of depth or length
cannot locate you, lightning bears you
everywhere, but nowhere within measure.
Death's a dummy played by dummy flesh
as, ever-ready, modern quintains spin;
systems endure, but forms must change forever;
human dust or petals, foetal folds,
vanish and reappear in later twilight
as ashes or next season's marigolds.

IV

What history tells are stories of the makers,
Shire lords, boundary over-runners,
manipulators of the priest and state.
The serf without the skill to raise
one standing oakwood god for guardian,
who could not plan a path to channel men,
was deftly cheated of archival heavens;
highwaymen took the purses, fervent prayers
were attributes of hard-embattled kings,
whose crimson records in the timelanes stand
like gaudy mirrors eye should focus on;
ark-low, they carve their earthly lettering,
ark-high, the undemanding miss the pages.

V

Yet, outside the tabernacle, on the waypath,
by evening horselanes, by the ghosts of knights,
see God within the Maids of Craft,
some snowbearded all-wise face
or by herbarium and spreading tree.
Some holy hand at outer level fills
man-forests with ark's fruitful essence;
above the evil flood-plains of the manors
the ark of sap spawns copies for the future
when crystal foresight greens those lands again.
A prize of hearts awaits the neophyte
- a home for rising consciousness displayed.

VI

Contemplate the flesh, its macrostructure,
its celled formality in cradle womb,
its chemical dusts deposited at death
in earthly strata, lakes, on ocean beds.
Upon the blueprint of etheric form
are drawn new phantom genes, predestined patterns
of new moulding needed by the species.
Shekhina power is vital in the egg.
Priest of four quarters and the slave of none,
masked by the brown Octobers of his thoughts,
man ventures on, his karma shoulder-slung.

Contemplate flesh, once of Word,
declared inviolate, else wrath
would follow like a locust wind.
Esau married a daughter of Elon
and desired Judith, daughter of Beeri.
By Melchizedek, king of Salem,
Priest of the Most High God,

172

the Divine Warrior entered his land
with loud obliterating curses,
trod the earth like a winepress of vengeance.
He who had mingled alien blood
with the flesh of the flesh of the father from Ur,
and sold for a mouthful of food his birthright,
broke with the faith of ancestors,
body meridian denied

VII

The path to soul vision is within;
inward light, body potential
near apotheosis is gained.
In the third eye's splendour
is a brotherhood with brilliance;
on the route to ultimate wisdom
the Abyss will not be recrossed;
in the glow of the high lamp
desire is revealed and then lost.

Yours is the jewel for the taking,
but beware of the shadow by your side,
the long forsaking of the golden chain;
fear the millennia, godhead denied
– karma, rebirth, ever-awakening
in cribs of earth-making, again and again.

APPENDIX

A. Extracts from *The Art Of Eric Ratcliffe,* by Brian Louis Pearce

The White River : "The poet has provided his own introduction in *Gleanings*......The greatest of all moments is perhaps that which is least dramatic and least expected, the first moment of a natural friendship, the moment of finding unaware a playmate near the river of dreams calling your name quietly in the face of the material claims of the world,holding out an object symbolic of hope......' "

The Green Man : "......explores that theme of a tree-god or tree-spirit to which he was to return in 1960 with **The Chronicle Of The Green Man**......it has, in places, the atmosphere of Tolkien's epic story *Lord Of The Rings*."

The Throw : "......too, creates a Tolkien-like world out of an experience as simple in origin, perhaps, as a day by the sea."

Death Was No Empty Hat : "......a quality of lightness and movement...... seems to imply that death is not necessarily something final or dreadful, but a swinging upward, as on a trapeze, to a richer and fuller life."

The Ragnarök Rocket Bomb : "The imagery is vivid but difficult......The author's love of......mythology and pre-history is well in evidence......continuous powerful stress gives an impressive hardness and strength to the poem......The outline of the bomb's effect can be traced in the long and magnificent passage, of a hard lyric intensity, commencing......'It has broken the bones of buried playmates......' a passage 38 lines in length."

The Suicides : "......strong in its rhythm and imagery......makes a compact impression whether read or heard. There is no rhyme. The lines are arranged, not by their number of syllables, but by the pattern of their stress. This pattern tends to be of 4 stresses to the line, although it is subtly varied, so as to avoid monotony. The stresses, like the

174

metaphors, tend to be very strong, and there is an underlying suggestion of Dylan Thomas in the style......It is not difficult to pick out the story, told with a moving simplicity, won through a complex art."

Listening Boy : "......direct and poignant......I would count it with **Elegy For My Uncle Buried At Girton** as one of his best and most moving elegiac poems."

Old Fragrance : "......a poem in 13 lines, which falls into three sections; the 1st ending with 'unborn' in the 4th line; the 2nd with 'dawn' in the 8th line, and the 3rd ending with 'corn'. In this way a formal structure is given to this very pleasant and evocative poem."

Mist On My Eyes : "Here is perhaps his most elaborate 'orchestration of idyllic archetypes', to quote from a letter of Geoffrey Holloway......Those who will read and re-read these poems......will find not only a growing understanding, but a deepening delight and appreciation."

Roman Silchester : "is a poem in 25 lines divided into paragraphs of 15 and 10 lines, respectively. It will be found that there is a natural pause after every 5th line, so that the poem is built in a more formal manner than might at first appear."

Mary And The Millwater Bells : "A most beautiful and appealing poem, clear and sustained, beautiful and evocative, and with a most delicate loveliness......In its mastery of technique, and in its power of music, image and association, it is not unlike 'Over Sir John's Hill' or 'Fern Hill'."

Stolen Property : "is in 3 stanzas, the two outer being of 9 lines and the middle section of 8 lines. The middle verse also contains one or two lines shorter in length than those of the two outer stanzas......The poem moves from consummation to motherhood and sonship, and traces the delicate sequence and continuity of image and experience through the generations......"

The Maiden Of The Moon's Boat : "5 lines, but like a poem of Li-Po, or a Noh play in a translation of Arthur Waley, its delicate pattern haunts the

175

mind."

A Lady Kneeling For Holy Communion : "The poet claims to find a relationship between the emotions that we experience in a pagan or pantheistic reaction to Nature and the 'vision inward' of the Christian experience."

The Golden Tempest : "has the 8:6 proportions of a sonnet, although the first 3 sections total 16 lines and the last section is of 12 lines, so that the actual number of lines in the poem is twice that of a sonnet, This is another archetypal poem......"

Elegy For My Uncle Buried At Girton : "......the last five lines, especially, create something of that same emotion merged with exultant vigour that we find toward the end of 'In The White Giant's Thigh'......one of E.R.'s most perennially satisfying poems."

The Unnecessary Silence : "suggests that, just as we misunderstand the beauty and meaning of life, and misuse it, so God may choose to misunderstand, and His misunderstanding would end in our destruction......The poem is in 6 verses, each of three lines. It rhymes AAB/CCD/EED/DFF/DGG/HII; showing a sort of cyclic return from the mid-point."

The Spirit Of The Green Light : "Here the past and present are merged, and are lost in the universal statement that speaks to our condition: the statement of the absolutes truth, goodness and beauty, that abide through the generations......The poem is in 7 verses, the 2nd, 4th and 6th being inset. 'Sing against blood' has the touch of Pound about it.

River Spy, 54 B.C. : "A carefully constructed poem, again with his familiar mood and atmosphere, each of its 3 stanzas commencing with the line 'O naked river spy'......Each 11-line stanza is extremely satisfying in structure and rhythm, and the narrative basis of the poem is easily followed."

B. Other comments

His best work has an original lyricism of exceptional character and beauty, showing great subtlety of image, rhythm and phrasing. At the same time he has created his own (mythical/historical) world. (BRIAN LOUIS PEARCE, in COMMIUS)

THE CHRONICLE OF THE GREEN MAN:
A primeval clarity. (DR. BRIAN HINTON, SOUTH ANTHOLOGY)

ARK:
A strong sequence filled with esoteric knowledge.
(MARGARET PAIN, WEYFARERS NEWSLETTER)

The abiding image for me, of these poems, is the use Ratcliffe makes of cradle and womb imagery. He links these deeply feminine images with death and rebirth, our spiritual journey which goes beyond death. (ANGELA TOPPING, ORE)

ADVENT:
A stunning long poem. (JOHN FRANCIS HAINES, NEW HOPE INTERNATIONAL REVIEW)

SCIENTARY:
A serious commentary on the cosmic principles of life which left me gasping because of its provoking penetration into our human state. (JOY O'BRIEN, ORE)

GHOSTS OF THE QUATERNARY:
...Lastly, a yearning attempt by the 'dead' narrator, to re-experience the loving relationship of a former life, drawing the lover to the place of his bones, irresistibly moving and beautiful. (JOY O'BRIEN, ORE)

177

LEO POEMS:
Eric Ratcliffe is at his best when describing women ...One feels that Mr. Ratcliffe's feeling for the past tends to cut him off from the present, so that he is left entombed in what is almost another world. (HEADLAND)

THE EXPERIMENT:
Demands of the reader a strong head for heights (and depths) ...a vast overview of the world from creation onwards, from the first forest predator to the boardroom variety, and sweep vertiginously from Roman legions to Thiepval on the Somme, and from King Arthur and Merlin to Marks and Sparks .... the general vision, though, is compulsive.......The highly prophetic tone is awesome and apposite to our times.....A challenging series... (FRANCES MARSHALL, IOTA)

A SUN-RED MANTLE:
His poetry is a mystical celebration of life, remote and unearthly....some of his images are obscure but elsewhere a clear joy shines through the symbolism. (R.M., RICHMOND AND TWICKENHAM TIMES)

COMMIUS:
.......Aneurin's Goddodin, a poem which in many ways it successfully recalls; the same relentless drive, heroic pride, soldierly speech and stark imagery. (WILLIAM IMRAY, NEW HOPE INTERNATIONAL REVIEW)

SCIENTARY:
I fancy a trip to the astral plane sometime, but the travel agents are unreliable. Meanwhile, there are holiday snaps ......(PETER CUDMORE, CHAPMAN)

I...assign ARK...and KINGDOMS to the junk pile, they promote the author's programme in lines of broken prose that never lift beyond the page. (JENNY ROBERTSON,CHAPMAN)